IT'S TIME TO TALK ABOUT ACES

DR. E'TOYARE MCDONALD-WILLIAMS

Printed in the United States of America
First Printing: August 2024
The Scribe Tribe Publishing Group

THE SCRIBE TRIBE
PUBLISHING GROUP

ISBN-978-1-958436-32-5 (print)
978-1-958436-33-2 (ebook)

Special Acknowledgements

It has been a long and challenging journey for my family and me. For the past four years, I have tried to find my place in education through several school districts, and each district's continued inequalities in education, employment, and representation in leadership positions are rooted in our country's shameful history of slavery and systemic racism. The Centers for Disease Control and Prevention (cdc.gov) recognizes racism as ACEs. This demeaning treatment motivated me to step out and pursue entrepreneurship for the 2023-2024 school year. This accomplishment would not have been possible without the grace of GOD, my Lord and savior Jesus Christ, and the encouragement, sacrifice, dedication, and loving support of my family and friends. To my parents and my three wonderful daughters Ker'Mari, Kynnedi, and Korri, who have shared in this journey with me, thank you for being my everyday motivation! Special thanks goes to my prayer warriors, my church: Concord Baptist Church, my Sorors of Delta Sigma Theta Sorority, Inc., Mag 07, my CORE Sorors, my step-team sisters, and my mentees near and far whom I still keep in touch with since 1995 until now. Thank you for being my motivation, my growth, my inspiration, my SUPPORT! My TR 2012-2020 crew never disappoints me. To see my educational impact through you humbles me. Each class holds a special place in my heart. I created Be Victorieus Foundation for you!

To my prayer warriors again, prayer is powerful. We serve an awesome God!-Phillipans 4:13

TABLE OF CONTENTS

IT'S TIME TO TALK ABOUT ACES!

As I embark on this journey through academia, research, and self-discovery, I am propelled by a singular commitment: to break the cycle of generational trauma and illuminate the path towards healing and resilience. My unwavering dedication to understanding and addressing the profound implications of Adverse Childhood Experiences (ACEs) serves as my guiding compass, guiding me through the uncharted territories of knowledge and discovery.

With each step forward, I am driven by a heartfelt sense of purpose—to contribute to a broader understanding of ACEs and their far-reaching effects on individuals, families, and communities. Yet, my journey extends beyond the confines of academia. It is a deeply personal quest rooted in empathy, compassion, and a relentless pursuit of social justice. By amplifying the voices of those affected by ACEs, I strive to foster empathy, understanding, and collective action towards creating trauma-informed systems of care and support.

As I navigate the complexities of this landscape, I understand how powerful knowledge can be, and I know that comes with a big responsibility. I am committed to leveraging my expertise to empower individuals, families, and communities to break free from the shackles of intergenerational trauma and forge a path towards healing and resilience. In this pursuit, I stand not as a solitary voyager but as a catalyst for change—a beacon of hope, guiding others towards a future defined by strength, resilience, and possibility.

For too long, the echoes of childhood trauma have resonated through the halls of our homes, schools, and communities, leaving a huge impact on the lives of countless individuals. In the sanctuary of homes, where love and safety should prevail, trauma has shattered the innocence of childhood. Abuse, neglect, violence and other adversities have left deep wounds on young hearts and minds. The scars of those experiences linger well into adulthood, shaping beliefs, behaviors, and relationships. These experiences are called adverse childhood experiences, better known as ACEs.

The effects of ACEs extend beyond the individual. It creates ripples that resonate throughout families and communities. The echoes of ACEs are an intense and far-reaching societal problem. It is a hidden epidemic that affects millions of people worldwide. It is a burden that we can no longer afford to ignore. We must break the cycle of trauma and create a world where all children can grow up in safe and nurturing environments.

To achieve this, we need to raise awareness about the prevalence and impact of ACEs. We need to educate professionals who work with children about the signs and symptoms of trauma, and we need to provide them with the tools and resources to help children heal. We also need to create supportive communities where children and families can feel safe and connected.

Breaking the cycle of ACEs is not for the weak; it is going to be an intense and demanding endeavor. It is going to be a process that is essential for creating a healthier and more just society. Again, it is not a task for the faint of heart. Breaking the cycle of ACEs, which already has a deep and lasting impact, will require a comprehensive and multifaceted approach that addresses the root causes of ACEs and provides support and resources to individuals, families, and communities. It involves creating safe and supportive environments, promoting healthy relationships, and implementing trauma-informed practices in various settings, such as schools, healthcare, and the criminal justice system.

One critical aspect of breaking the cycle of ACEs is recognizing and addressing the intergenerational transmission of trauma. Children who grow up in households where trauma is present are more likely to experience ACEs themselves, continuing the cycle. Therefore, interventions aimed at preventing ACEs must consider the family context and provide support to parents and caregivers. Breaking the cycle of ACEs will require addressing the social and economic factors that contribute to trauma. Poverty, discrimination, lack of access to healthcare and education, and community violence are all risk factors for ACEs. By addressing these root causes, we can create a more equitable society where all children have the opportunity to thrive.

Breaking the cycle of ACEs is a long-term commitment that requires collaboration among individuals, families, communities, and policymakers. It involves changing societal norms, promoting resilience, and creating a culture of understanding and support. By working together, we can create a world where every child has the chance to reach their full potential, free from the burden of ACEs. By working together, we can ensure that all children have the opportunity to reach their full potential and live lives free from the lingering shadows of trauma. Now, as we stand at the precipice of understanding, empathy, and healing, it is time to cast aside the shadows and initiate a conversation that is long overdue.

Creating victory among individuals through understanding ACEs is a transformative journey that not only promotes personal healing but also contributes to the well-being of communities. By understanding ACEs and their far-reaching effects, we embark on a journey of empowerment and enlightenment that holds the potential to break the cyclical nature of generational trauma. Creating victory means we not only confront our own past experiences and uncover the fascinating story of our family's past, but we recognize how it shapes our present and influences our future. By shedding light on the shadows of our past, we pave the way for healing and growth, not only for ourselves but for those around us.

Understanding ACEs fosters empathy and compassion as we come to realize that the struggles we face are not isolated incidents but shared experiences woven into the fabric of our society. It empowers us to reach out to others with empathy, understanding, and support, creating a network of resilience that uplifts and strengthens us all. Addressing ACEs and the underlying trauma means we take proactive steps towards preventing adverse outcomes and fostering healthier, more nurturing environments for future generations. We become agents of change, breaking free from the constraints of the past and forging a path towards a brighter, more hopeful future.

As I invite you to join me on this journey, I offer not just my story but a shared narrative of resilience, courage, and healing. Together, we explore the depths of generational trauma, confront its lingering effects, and embrace the transformative power of breaking free from the chains that bind us. In doing so, we pave the way for personal growth, collective healing, and the creation of a more compassionate and supportive world for all.

Understanding ACEs is a step towards breaking the cycle of generational trauma, fostering empathy, preventing adverse outcomes, and building resilient, supportive environments for individuals to thrive. As I embarked on my journey through life, I found myself unknowingly taking on the role of a cyclebreaker. Growing up, I was exposed to countless stories that seemed to echo a common theme. Over two decades of comprehensive research, both within the United States and other countries, have consistently revealed a striking correlation between the number of ACEs an individual faces as a child and the likelihood of encountering various health, mental, social, and behavioral challenges throughout their life span. These difficulties can continue into adulthood and even be passed down to future generations.

Understanding the relationship between ACEs and long-term outcomes has far-reaching implications for public health, education, and social policy. By raising awareness about ACEs and the importance of early childhood experiences, we can work collectively to create a society where all children have the opportunity to thrive and reach their full potential. Let's join forces and really dig into ACEs, shall we? By doing so, we can help people and communities, raise awareness about ACEs, and make the world a more compassionate and resilient place for everyone. Together, we can make a real difference!

Everyone has a story, right? As I share my story, I invite you to join me on this relatable journey—a journey that explores the depths of generational trauma, the complexities of family history, and the transformative power of breaking free from the chains that bind us. Here I am to share with you my story of what led me to find ACEs in my role as a cycle breaker who broke generational curses as a first generation high school graduate to a narrative for me, Dr. Victorieus, a cycle breaker who found purpose in mentorship, resilience, and the pursuit of a collective healing journey. It's time to talk about ACEs and create victory for yourself and become VicTORIEus in your journey towards healing!

CHAPTER 1

BREAK THE CYCLE OF GENERATIONAL TRAUMA

Trauma isn't just something that comes and goes; it's something that touches every part of our lives. Trauma, in its essence, is a response to an overwhelming and deeply distressing event or experience that overloads our capacity to cope. It can be a single incident such as a natural disaster, accident, or violent crime, or it can be a series of chronic stressors such as childhood abuse or neglect. Trauma, no matter what shape or size, can really mess with our feeling of safety and make us feel all alone and exposed.

One of the key mechanisms through which trauma exerts its influence is by disrupting the normal functioning of our brain. When we experience trauma, the brain's stress response system goes into overdrive, flooding us with hormones such as cortisol and adrenaline. These hormones can have a profound impact on our emotions, thoughts, and behaviors, making us feel anxious, irritable, and hypervigilant. Over time, chronic exposure to stress hormones can lead to changes in brain structure and function, making us more susceptible to mental health problems such as depression, anxiety, and post-traumatic stress disorder (PTSD). Trauma can also have a huge impact on our relationships and social functioning. When we have experienced trauma, we may find it difficult to trust others or form close attachments.

We may also withdraw from social activities and isolate ourselves from the people we care about. This can lead to feelings of loneliness, isolation, and a sense of disconnection from the world around us. Lastly, trauma can have a ripple effect on our physical health. Research has shown that people who have experienced trauma are at increased risk for a range of health problems including, heart disease, stroke, diabetes, and autoimmune disorders. This is likely due to the fact that trauma can lead to chronic inflammation, which is a major risk factor for many diseases.

The implications of trauma for mental health and well-being are huge and extensive. Trauma can lead to a range of psychiatric disorders, including depression, anxiety, PTSD, and substance abuse. It can also impair our ability to function in our daily lives, making it difficult to hold a job, maintain relationships, or participate in social activities. In severe cases, trauma can even lead to suicide. It is important to note that not everyone who experiences trauma will develop mental health problems. However, those who are exposed to trauma are at an increased risk. There are a number of factors that can influence the likelihood of developing mental health problems after trauma, including the severity and duration of the trauma, the person's coping skills, and the availability of social support.

Understanding your trauma and how it's linked to ACEs isn't going to be a walk in the park. It's like this huge, complicated puzzle that needs a bunch of different pieces to come together so that you can see the bigger picture. Education plays a crucial role in empowering healthcare professionals with the knowledge and understanding of the impact that ACEs have on health outcomes. Equipping them with trauma-informed care practices will enable them to provide more effective and compassionate care to individuals who have experienced ACEs.

Additionally, raising awareness about ACEs and trauma in the broader community is essential. Public education campaigns, media portrayals, and community forums can help reduce the stigma surrounding trauma and create a more understanding and supportive environment. By dispelling misconceptions and promoting accurate information, we can encourage individuals to seek help and access the resources they need. Promoting trauma-informed care in various settings, including schools, workplaces, and healthcare systems is paramount. This involves creating safe and supportive environments that recognize the impact of trauma on individuals' lives. Trauma-informed care practices prioritize respect, empathy, and understanding, ensuring that individuals feel safe and empowered to share their experiences. To ensure the well-being and resilience of individuals who have experienced ACEs, it is crucial to provide accessible and comprehensive support. This can include mental health services, counseling, peer support groups, and community-based programs. By offering a range of resources and services, we can cater to the diverse needs of individuals and help them build coping mechanisms, develop resilience, and thrive in their lives.

Addressing the issue of an unfamiliar, multifaceted approach requires collaboration among various stakeholders to ensure comprehensive understanding and implementation. Here's an elaborated explanation of the roles each stakeholder group can play in creating a more informed, compassionate, and trauma-sensitive society:

Healthcare Professionals:

- **Education and Awareness Campaigns:** Healthcare professionals, including doctors, nurses, social workers, and mental health counselors, can play a crucial role in educating the public about trauma and ACEs through workshops, seminars, and community outreach programs.
- **Trauma-Informed Care Training:** Healthcare professionals should receive training in trauma-informed care, which involves

understanding the impact of trauma on individuals and adopting practices that promote safety, empowerment, and respect.

- **Screening for ACEs:** Healthcare professionals can routinely screen patients for ACEs using validated questionnaires. This screening enables early identification of individuals who may benefit from trauma-focused interventions.

- **Trauma-Sensitive Treatment:** Healthcare professionals should be equipped to provide trauma-sensitive treatment, such as cognitive-behavioral therapy, trauma-focused therapy, and eye movement desensitization and reprocessing (EMDR).

Educators:

- **Trauma-Informed Education:** Educators can incorporate trauma-informed practices into the educational system, creating a safe and supportive environment for students who have experienced trauma.

- **Mental Health Education:** Educators can include mental health and trauma education in the curriculum, helping students develop coping mechanisms and resilience.

- **Trauma-Sensitive Discipline:** Educators should adopt trauma-sensitive discipline approaches that focus on understanding the underlying causes of student behavior rather than relying on punitive measures.

Community Leaders:

- **Community Awareness Campaigns:** Community leaders, such as religious leaders, community organizers, and local government officials, can raise awareness about trauma and ACEs through public forums, town halls, and community events.

- **Resource Mapping:** Community leaders can map out available resources for trauma survivors, such as mental health services, support groups, and crisis hotlines, and make this information easily accessible to the public.
- **Trauma-Informed Community Programs:** Community leaders can establish trauma-informed programs, such as after-school programs, community gardens, and recreational activities that provide a safe and supportive environment for individuals affected by trauma.

Policymakers:

- **Trauma-Informed Policy Development:** Policymakers can develop trauma-informed policies that address the needs of individuals who have experienced trauma. This includes policies related to healthcare, education, housing, and criminal justice.
- **Funding for Trauma-Related Services:** Policymakers can allocate funding for trauma-related services, such as trauma therapy, support groups, and research on trauma and resilience.
- **Trauma-Sensitive Legislation:** Policymakers can enact legislation that protects the rights of trauma survivors and provides access to appropriate care and support.

By working together, these stakeholders can help create a society that is more informed, compassionate, and trauma-sensitive. This will ultimately lead to improved outcomes for individuals who have experienced trauma, allowing them to overcome the challenges they face and achieve their full potential by breaking the cycle of trauma.

Discussing ACEs can be emotionally challenging and triggering. Childhood trauma often involves sensitive and painful memories, making it difficult for individuals to share their experiences. Fear of judgment, stigma, or shame can also contribute to the reluctance to talk about ACEs. Additionally, societal pressure to project strength and resilience may discourage individuals from admitting vulnerability and seeking support. The stigma surrounding mental health issues further complicates the situation. The lack of awareness and stigma surrounding ACEs can have far-reaching consequences for individuals' physical and mental well-being. It can contribute to delayed diagnoses, inadequate treatment, and increased healthcare costs. It can also lead to social isolation, relationship difficulties, and decreased productivity at work or school. The cycle of ACEs perpetuates itself when individuals who have experienced trauma in childhood are more likely to experience trauma in adulthood, which in turn increases the risk of their children experiencing ACEs. This cycle can span generations, leading to a perpetuation of trauma and its associated negative consequences.

My ACEs cycle involves a span unveiling generational trauma that led to years of being reluctant to discuss my experiences due to fear of being labeled or misunderstood.

Over the years, this created a complex web of emotional and psychological challenges. For many individuals, myself included, navigating the aftermath of such experiences can be fraught with reluctance and apprehension. People are terrified of being criticized or misunderstood. This fear comes from all sorts of places. There is the fear of societal stigma and judgment, where discussing ACEs may lead to being unfairly categorized or ostracized. Society's misconceptions about trauma and mental health can make those fears worse, causing individuals to feel isolated and ashamed of their experiences.

There's the fear of personal vulnerability and emotional exposure. Opening up about ACEs means delving into deeply personal and often painful memories, which can evoke a sense of rawness and vulnerability. There's a fear of being judged or dismissed, having one's experiences minimized or invalidated by others who may not fully understand the depth of trauma endured. There is also the fear of triggering further trauma or retraumatization. Revisiting past experiences can unearth buried emotions and memories, stirring up feelings of distress or anguish. The prospect of reliving traumatic events, even in the context of healing, can be overwhelming and intimidating, leading individuals to avoid discussing their experiences altogether.

In the face of these fears, many individuals may choose to remain silent, keeping their ACEs hidden beneath a veil of secrecy and shame. However, it's essential to recognize that this reluctance to discuss ACEs is a natural response to the complex and deeply ingrained effects of trauma. It's a survival mechanism, born out of a need to protect oneself from further harm.

This stigma has acted as a barrier, preventing me from seeking the support and resources that could have helped me break the cycle of silence and isolation that has plagued my life. My unwillingness to open up about my childhood experiences had a huge impact. I missed out on opportunities for healing and growth, and my physical and mental health suffered. The cycle of silence and isolation became a self-fulfilling prophecy.

Where the imprints of trauma linger across generations, fostering greater awareness and understanding is an imperative. To this end, creating safe and supportive spaces becomes paramount, environments where individuals can feel empowered to share their experiences without the fear of judgment or retribution. By breaking the silence that often shrouds ACEs, we unlock the potential for healing and resilience.

It's time to talk about ACEs! Imagine a world where individuals are no longer burdened by the shame and stigma associated with ACEs. A world where they can openly discuss their experiences, knowing that they will be met with compassion, empathy, and a genuine desire to understand. This is the vision we strive to realize, a world where the tangled threads of generational trauma are unraveled, making way for newfound strength and resilience. Achieving this vision requires a collective effort. It begins with educating ourselves about ACEs, their prevalence, and their profound impact on individuals, families, and communities. Armed with this knowledge, we can become agents of change, creating ripples of awareness that spread throughout society.

It's time to talk about ACEs! The myths and misconceptions surrounding ACEs have perpetuated a culture of shame and silence, hindering individuals from seeking help or discussing their experiences. By fostering an open and honest dialogue, we can shatter these barriers and create a culture of understanding and acceptance, where individuals feel safe to share their stories without fear of being marginalized or dismissed. Elevating awareness and understanding of ACEs is not just an act of compassion; it holds immense value for the well-being of individuals, families, and communities.

When we acknowledge the impact of ACEs, we recognize that trauma experienced in childhood can have lasting consequences on physical, mental, and emotional health throughout adulthood. Research has established strong links between ACEs and chronic health conditions, mental health disorders, addiction, and risky behaviors. By addressing ACEs, we can potentially reduce the prevalence of these issues, leading to healthier individuals and communities. The time for action is now! By eliminating the stigma associated with ACEs, promoting open dialogue, and investing in evidence-based prevention and intervention programs, we can create a society that is trauma-informed and supportive, where individuals feel safe to heal and reach their full potential. It's time to talk about ACEs!

How did I become Victorieus?

When the opportunity to fulfill my dream of becoming the first person from both sides of my family to pursue my doctorate degree was presented to me, I was excited yet nervous. It was a huge deal, and I knew it would change my life in a big way. I've always loved learning and exploring new things. That's why I was so excited to start my doctoral program. But I was also a little bit scared. Married with three children and working full-time as a case manager, an educator as well as the Director of Student Activities, I knew it was going to be a lot of work, and I wasn't sure if I was up for the challenge. However, I was determined to make my family proud and to set a good example for my girls. So, I took a deep breath and stepped into the unknown.

The statement of purpose, initially perceived as a requirement for admission, turned out to be a powerful tool for personal and professional transformation. It set the stage for a journey that challenged me intellectually, expanded my horizons, and shaped me into the scholar and professional I am today. In crafting my statement of purpose, I articulated not only my academic ambitions but it made me think a lot about my own life. It was like going on a journey down memory lane, thinking about all the ups and downs I had been through, and how they shaped me into the person I am today. Little did I realize that those carefully chosen words would serve as a roadmap for the years to come—a roadmap that guided me through the rigors of coursework, propelled me through research endeavors, and fueled my commitment to make a meaningful impact in the field of psychology. The statement of purpose, once confined to a few pages, metamorphosed into a guiding manifesto, anchoring me in moments of doubt and propelling me forward during times of uncertainty.

As I embarked on my doctoral journey at Chicago State University, that initial statement of purpose became a compass, steering me through the uncharted territories of academia, research, and self-discovery. It was the proclamation of my commitment to break the cycle of generational trauma and to contribute to a broader understanding of its implications on young adults. In retrospect, my statement of purpose was not just an admission requirement; it was the seed that sprouted into a deep and satisfying learning journey. The statement of purpose, crafted with intention and passion, has been the catalyst for every achievement, every breakthrough, and every milestone reached during my doctoral pursuit. It captures the essence of my journey—a journey that began with a simple declaration but has since evolved into a transformative exploration of knowledge, resilience, and the burning desire to unravel the complexities of the pursuit of breaking generational cycles. A journey that would lead me to examine the intricate relationship between Adverse Childhood Experiences (ACEs) and participation in extracurricular activities in young adults.

My Statement of Purpose

Chicago State University
Doctoral Studies Application
Statement of Purpose
Applicant: Mrs. E'Toyare Williams

As I sat and pondered about what I wanted to use as a basis for my statement of purpose, I realized that we all were all students once upon a time. I have given a lot of thought into pursuing my doctorate degree. When reaching my decision, I have included some of my personal goals because I feel that those goals set the basis for me and are the tools needed in order to succeed in an ever-changing environment. I became a teacher because there was no "me" out there for me to "go to" for help. There is so much that has happened in my life that has helped me reach this decision to pursue my doctorate. However, all of this has shaped me into the educator that I am today. If I knew what I know now about my educational goals then maybe I could have taken my education to another level at that particular time— looking, of course, in hindsight.

I was born and raised in Kansas City, Missouri and attended schools in the city school system, graduating from Paseo Academy of Visual and Performing Arts High School in 1995. At that time, I accomplished a goal that my parents had set for me, which was to become a first generation high school graduate and college student. While it was a goal for my parents to earn their high school diploma, it was not something that they had an opportunity to realize; thus, accomplishing that feat became not just a personal endeavor but a family milestone. I was raised to believe that education is very important and to take it very seriously. That is one of the several personal reasons why I am pursuing my doctorate degree. I felt the desire to continue due to the motivation from my family and friends who did not get the chance to accomplish the same goals. Now that I am a married mother of three girls, I want to instill the same values to my children.

I graduated from Central Missouri State University, where I received a Bachelor of Science in Psychology in May of 1999. Soon thereafter, I took a job as a manager. However, it took me five years before I realized that I was in the wrong field and going down the wrong

career path. I left my position as a manager and decided to follow my heart, which was to educate our youth. While it was always a dream to pursue my masters degree, I have always considered myself to be a "people person" and one who motivates others. It becomes apparent more and more everyday that I have made the right choice to work in the field of education. While the flames and my motivations are driving me to reach my goals, I plan on pursuing my education further by challenging myself in pursuit of my doctorate degree in Educational Leadership. Even after a trying day, I still look forward to teaching and seeing my students the next day.

While pursuing my teaching degree at National-Louis University, I was given the opportunity to pursue my masters degree in Business Administration. I took full advantage of being employed by the University of Phoenix as a recruiter. When working with the potential candidates, the desire to teach was always there. Thus, the changes to my personal and professional goals gave me the push I needed to finish my master of art degree in teaching five years later. I have been teaching ever since!

Utilizing your knowledge and expertise all depends on your current situation. It can be a tool that can be used to have a positive impact on your life regardless of previous decisions made. I consider myself a very hard worker, willing to go the extra mile in order to become successful.

If I am chosen as a doctoral candidate, I plan to take on a full course load, as well as work full-time in my current position as the Director of Student Activities at Thornridge High School. I will spend the majority of my leisure time maintaining focus on my class work so that I will not fall behind schedule. I will study, keep up with readings, and write notes for papers for the classes that I take at every available moment.

I have no plans at all to leave the field of education. The desire and my motivation will always stoke a fire in my heart. I feel that if I continue in the education setting, I may be able to set the same flame that continues to burn in my heart in the students I serve today. In addition to Director of Student Activities, I am also a special education teacher. My willingness to teach students with special needs comes from the heart. I believe that all students deserve a chance and should be treated like everyone else. Teaching students with special needs has already placed me in a position that has helped me grow and develop in my professional career. I believe that I have the motivation to educate our youth. I apply every concept and lessons that are taught by my past and current professors at University of Central Missouri, University of Phoenix and National-Louis University in the classroom to better help me become a successful teacher and a positive role model. I have the desire to teach, and my motivation stays strong through the help of my family, friends and the students that I come in contact with on a daily basis. Education is a recycling process, and I want to be the one that helps our future make the best decisions possible—in school and in their lives.

As I continue to grow both personally and professionally, I believe that each of these goals has played a significant role in typifying my character that has made me utilize these values in every aspect of my life. I still have a lot to learn, but goals and values are inherited- not learned. Even though I tend to stick with my personal goals more than the other goals, all of my goals can be implemented in my professional environment and will continue to enhance my character and motivate me to be successful.

Understanding ACEs can allow individuals to recognize patterns of generational trauma and work towards breaking the cycle. By addressing and healing from ACEs, people can prevent the transmission of trauma to future generations, fostering a healthier family legacy.

As I embarked upon my educational journey to become the first person on both sides of my family to receive my doctorate degree, I was driven by a desire to honor my family and make them proud. I was still unaware of the profound impact that their childhood trauma had on my own life after all of these years. Growing up, I was unaware that childhood trauma even had a name. You could not ask any questions about it either. I was always told to "stay out of grown folks business." It was only years later pursuing my doctorate degree as I reflected on my own experiences with childhood trauma growing up that I came to recognize the ways in which my parents' childhood trauma had shaped my own childhood and adolescence. I had often struggled with the emotional turmoil stemming from my childhood trauma. The scars of household dysfunction left deep wounds that shaped my perceptions and behaviors. However, it was not until I dug into my own research that started in a psychology class at the University of Central Missouri in Warrensburg, Mo. in pursuit of my bachelor's degree that I understood the profound impact of my parents' childhood trauma on their parenting style and, consequently, on my own upbringing.

In pursuit of understanding my own ACEs, I added my Masters degree in Business Administration and my Masters degree in Teaching to my list of life's experiences, recognizing the diverse skill sets and perspectives they both bring to my personal and professional growth. These degrees are not just credentials but represent significant investments of time and effort in acquiring valuable knowledge and skills. However, through these academic endeavors, I started to understand the extreme impact of my students' childhood trauma on their own education.

It was not until I delved deeper into my research for my doctorate degree, I discovered the profound impact that my parents' ACEs had on their parenting style, and subsequently, on my own upbringing as well. It became evident that the scars of their past experiences had shaped the way they approached parenthood, often passing down patterns and behaviors that were rooted in their own unresolved trauma. I discovered that those experiences had a name. Since 1998, evidence has demonstrated the prevalence of different types of adverse or potentially traumatizing experiences, commonly referred to as ACEs, that can happen during childhood. ACEs can include physical, emotional, or sexual abuse; physical, sexual and emotional neglect; household dysfunction and other adversities, such as community violence and bullying. They are alarmingly common, with studies suggesting that up to two-thirds of children in the United States have experienced at least one ACE and that more than one in five have experienced three or more.1 The repercussions of ACEs extend to physical health outcomes, contributing to a heightened risk of chronic conditions. Studies have shown a correlation between ACEs and an increased likelihood of developing heart disease, stroke, and certain types of cancer in adulthood. Not understanding ACEs early in life can really mess with your body's stress response and other biological processes. This can set you up for health problems later on in life!

When it comes to society as a whole, the effects of ACEs aren't just about how people feel; they reach into all sorts of areas of life. Individuals who have experienced ACEs may face an elevated risk of social problems such as poverty, unemployment, and involvement in criminal activities. The connection between early adversity and socio-economic struggles underscores the complex interplay between personal experiences and broader societal outcomes. ACEs can create a cycle that affects not only the individual but also their community and society overall. The implications of exposure to ACEs are profound and enduring, shaping mental, physical, and social dimensions of adulthood. It's super important to understand how tough times in childhood can affect people in the long run. If we want

---

1 - https://thrivingschools.kaiserpermanente.org/mental-health/aces/

to help people who've had a rough start, we need to come up with ways to lessen the long-term effects and help them bounce back.

The knowledge I gained doing research shed light on the difficulties my parents faced in forming healthy relationships. Their early experiences left them with deep-seated emotional wounds that hindered their ability to connect with others in a secure and fulfilling way. This manifested in various ways, such as difficulty in expressing emotions, setting boundaries, and trusting others, which led to the understanding of our ACEs under the "Household Dysfunction" umbrella. The discovery created a bunch of challenges that became apparent in my own life. I realized how much ACEs affected me; it was like a light bulb went off. It made sense why I was struggling with so much at such an early age! This allowed me to trace my parents' roots back to the experiences of their past.

Growing up, showing emotions wasn't really a thing, so I never really knew how to handle my feelings. It was like I was walking through a maze, not knowing which way to turn. I came to understand the concept of emotional dysregulation, a common symptom of childhood trauma. My parents often struggled to manage their emotions, swinging between extremes of intense anger, sadness, and anxiety. Our family was like a rollercoaster ride of emotions, always unpredictable and sometimes out of control. The trauma my parents had experienced in their youth had created a blueprint for their own parenting style. Without realizing it, they continued to do things and act in ways that had been handed down from their parents.

The bittersweet moment of realization also marked a turning point in my understanding of my parents and my relationship with them. While it brought to light the challenges they had faced, it also fostered a deeper connection built on empathy and compassion. Equipped with this knowledge, I could navigate the complexities of our family dynamics with greater understanding and seek ways to break the cycle of trauma, paving the way for healing and growth. On the one hand, I felt a sense of compassion and understanding for my parents, recognizing that their behavior was not always intentional or malicious. On the other hand, it brought to light the complex and sometimes painful legacy of intergenerational trauma. I understood that the effects of my parents' childhood trauma had not only shaped their parenting but had also influenced my own experiences and emotional development. By understanding the impact of my parents' past experiences in my own life, I began the healing journey to break free from the cycle of trauma to create a more positive and healthy future for myself and for my family.

Knowledge of ACEs fosters empathy and compassion among individuals. When people understand the impact of childhood trauma on others, they are more likely to approach relationships with understanding, patience, and empathy, contributing to a supportive and nurturing community.

CHAPTER 2

PROMOTING EMPATHY AND COMPASSION

As educators, we were introduced to the concept of ACEs during a professional development session. During the professional development session, we learned about the different types of ACEs and their potential consequences. We also discussed the importance of creating a supportive and nurturing environment for our students to help prevent ACEs from occurring. We explored various strategies and resources that we could implement in our classrooms and schools to promote the well-being of our students. It was an eye-opening experience for me because it brought awareness to the profound impact that ACEs can have on children's well-being. Learning about the possible long-term effects made me realize how important teachers are in creating a supportive and nurturing environment that highlighted the importance of a holistic approach to education. It moved beyond academics to acknowledge the crucial role that emotional and social well-being play in a student's overall development. The highlight for me was the influential role that educators play in the lives of their students. As an educator, the potential to be a positive force in shaping the emotional and social landscape for students, contributing to their overall resilience and ability to cope with challenges was what I was already doing in my previous position as Director of Student Activities.

The professional development session from the district provided a wealth of actionable strategies and resources that I immediately incorporated in my position. Practical tips on creating a welcoming environment, establishing positive relationships with students and staff, and promoting resilience in the face of adversity were particularly impactful. These strategies align with my goal of fostering a space where all students feel safe, respected, and capable of reaching their full potential. By understanding the potential impact of ACEs, I became a compassionate and supportive figure in the lives of the students. Already mentoring students in my previous positions as an educator, I also realized that I have the opportunity to create a positive and nurturing atmosphere where students feel valued, heard, and empowered to overcome adversity due to their ACEs.

Overall, the professional development session was another valuable tool to help promote passion and empathy with my students. I was always committed to fostering a positive and nurturing learning environment where all students thrive and reach their full potential, and that is when I decided I would incorporate my mentorship into practice for all of my students, whether they were in my classroom or participated in activities in the school. I wanted to make sure that every student had the opportunity to participate in extracurricular activities. I wanted to make sure that I served as a positive role model who could provide guidance, support, and encouragement to individuals who lacked positive adult influences in their lives due to ACEs. Mentorship in addition to the Activity Director position allowed students to learn from someone who overcame similar challenges and could provide valuable insights and perspectives that the student could understand. I truly believe it was because of my understanding of ACEs that I connected with so many students over the years and now it was time to put it into practice.

While searching for research for dissertation completion, Dr. Nadine Burke Harris' TED talk on ACEs also served as a profound revelation, shedding light on aspects of my own childhood that had long lingered in the shadows. Her compelling insights and research not only provided a framework to comprehend the impact of early-life adversity but also offered a lens through which I could finally make sense of my own experiences. Dr. Burke Harris' empathy and compassion as she educated us all through her TED Talk still sends chills every time I watch it! Her discussion on the cumulative effects of ACEs, spanning from household dysfunction to abuse and neglect, resonated deeply with me. As she unraveled the science behind the physiological responses to stress during childhood, I found myself connecting the dots between her findings and the emotions that had lingered within me for years. One crucial aspect that Dr. Burke Harris highlighted was the long-term health consequences of untreated childhood trauma. This struck a chord as I began to recognize parallels between her descriptions and my own health journey. The link between childhood adversity and increased risk of various health issues became a pivotal revelation, offering an explanation for challenges I had faced but struggled to understand.

Her emphasis on the importance of early intervention and the role of a supportive community underscored the significance of seeking help and building a network of understanding individuals. It encouraged me to reevaluate my own path to healing and consider the potential benefits of seeking professional support. Dr. Nadine Burke Harris' TED Talk became a catalyst for self-reflection and understanding. It provided me with a language to articulate the impact of my early experiences and validated the complexities of navigating my own childhood trauma which officially was given a name–Adverse Childhood Experiences.

Armed with this new-found knowledge, I felt empowered to embark on a journey of healing and resilience, armed with a greater understanding of the profound effects of ACEs on my life. I was also in the middle of developing a topic for my dissertation. None of the topics that I shared with my professor resonated until I was introduced to ACEs. My professor was excited that I finally found a topic that also ignited my own empathy and compassion on a professional and personal level and that is when the journey to dissertation began.

I included the information provided to me through the professional development from work and continued to learn about ACEs through research and reading requirements for class completion. I started to attend conferences and workshops on the topic. I knew by staying informed about ACEs, I could not only support my students and help them to reach their full potential, but I could help myself by fostering a deeper understanding of the complexities of trauma.

Through required research and learning more about ACEs, I was blown away by how much it affects all of us! Armed with this knowledge, I felt a responsibility to create a supportive environment for my students, one that recognizes and addresses the challenges stemming from their childhood trauma. The more I learned, the more I became convinced of the urgency to spread awareness about ACEs. It was not just about understanding my students; it was about advocating for a broader societal shift in how we approach trauma and mental health. By gathering a better understanding of ACEs, I realized I could help my students do better in school and also contribute to the bigger conversation about mental health and well-being.

Awareness of ACEs empowers individuals to prioritize mental and emotional well-being. By understanding the potential impact of childhood trauma on mental health, people can seek appropriate support, engage in self-care practices, and promote emotional resilience.

CHAPTER 3

ENHANCING MENTAL AND EMOTIONAL WELL-BEING

Through my studies, I learned that the cycle of trauma can perpetuate across generations. Parental trauma, often stemming from ACEs can manifest in various ways, including inconsistent parenting, emotional neglect, or even abuse. Recognizing this intergenerational transmission of trauma allowed me to gain a deeper understanding of my parents' behaviors and the challenges they faced in raising me.

I realized that the effects of childhood trauma extend beyond the individual. It can have a ripple effect, shaping family dynamics, relationships, and the overall trajectory of lives. My parents' childhood trauma had not only impacted their parenting but also influenced their communication patterns, conflict resolution strategies, and emotional expressiveness within our family. Equipped with this understanding, I embarked on a journey of self-discovery, therapy, and education, aiming to unravel the complexities of trauma and its lasting effects through my dissertation. I also realized as an educator that the experiences of childhood trauma I endured growing up were the same experiences that students confided in me with. It was a huge revelation!

In essence, my journey into discovering ACEs became a transformative cycle of learning, implementing, and advocating. Understanding ACEs deepened my understanding of the challenges that some of our students may be facing. It has also helped me develop a greater sense of empathy and compassion for students. I realized that being aware of ACEs, I could better support our students and create a more positive and inclusive learning environment for all. What I had long dismissed as simply the challenges of growing up took on a new significance as I began to understand the effects of childhood trauma. I discovered that our experiences, marked by neglect, emotional abuse, and a lack of consistent nurturing, were not the norm. They were the manifestations of a trauma that had been passed down through generations.

The more I learned about childhood trauma, the more I realized that it had not only affected my family but also left a deep imprint on my own life. It shaped my relationships, my coping mechanisms, and my understanding of the world. With this new awareness, I began a quest of healing and self-discovery. I sought professional help, engaged in therapy, and surrounded myself with supportive friends who understood the complexities of my experiences. Through this process, I began to unravel the threads of my past, finding both pain and resilience along the way.

Embracing my own story required confronting uncomfortable truths about my past. Acknowledging the existence of ACEs involves revisiting difficult memories and acknowledging the impact of those experiences on my life. It was really tough for me to do this because it meant showing a side of myself that I don't usually show. I would also require myself to revisit those questions I could not ask when I was a kid because I had to stay out of grown folks' business. It meant that I had to overcome those internal barriers, challenge societal stigmas, and recognize that ACEs are not a reflection of personal failure but rather a result of challenging circumstances that were not under my control.

Diving into my own story involved navigating a range of emotions from pain and sadness to anger and frustration. It allowed me to understand the generational impact of ACEs on my own family. Recognizing how trauma was passed down through generations was a crucial step in breaking the cycle, as it provides insight into patterns that need to be disrupted for the sake of my own healing and future generations. Acceptance of my own story was a powerful form of self-empowerment for me. It involved acknowledging that my experiences are part of my journey but do not define my worth or potential, which served as a foundation for growth and transformation. Getting to know yourself better is all about embracing your own story. It's like piecing together a puzzle and seeing how it all fits! It allows you to connect the dots between past experiences and current challenges, fostering self-awareness and paving the way for intentional healing. People with childhood trauma often thrive in silence, and breaking that silence is a courageous act.

As I continued searching for research, I realized I was making a difference in breaking down the barriers around talking about ACEs, which supported my personal healing journey through therapy. I learned that sharing my story can create connections with others who have faced similar challenges. This sense of connection and shared experience fosters a supportive community, offering understanding and encouragement along the healing journey. By openly discussing my experiences and the process of healing, I realized that I was contributing to breaking the stigma surrounding ACEs. Ultimately, embracing my story was a key step in shattering the cycle of trauma and creating a different future for myself and my family.

Understanding my past enables me to make intentional choices that contribute to a healthier, more positive legacy for the generations to come.

While embracing my own story proved to be a challenging and emotionally demanding process, it was a necessary step for understanding, acceptance, and ultimately, healing. It was a transformative journey that empowered me to break the cycle of trauma, fostering a future characterized by resilience, strength, and positive change.

Those who understand ACEs can apply this knowledge to enhance parenting and caregiving practices. Recognizing the effects of trauma helps individuals create a safe and nurturing environment for children, breaking the cycle of adverse experiences and promoting healthy development.

CHAPTER 4

IMPROVING PARENTING AND CAREGIVING PRACTICES

I came from Edrick McDonald and Edna Slaughter-McDonald. Both of my parents were raised by their fathers. My father lost his mother recovering from a surgery as a teenager. My mother lost her mother from abandonment as a toddler. Both of my grandfathers remarried. My paternal grandfather married 3 times, my maternal grandfather married 8 times. Yes, eight times! I had a LOT of cousins growing up! If you have never heard of generational trauma before, I just provided a great example of what generational trauma looks like. Generational trauma are traumatic events that occur decades prior to the current generation and have had an impact on the way that individuals understand, cope with, and heal from trauma. Growing up without a mother for both of my parents was a traumatic experience within itself! Although there is no specific diagnosis of generational trauma, according to the Diagnostic and Statistical Manual of Mental Disorders, Fifth Edition (DSM-5), generational trauma may not be formally classified in diagnostic manuals like the DSM-5. The existence and impact of generational trauma are recognized within the mental health community and beyond. Understanding and addressing generational trauma requires a comprehensive approach that considers historical, cultural, familial, and individual factors, with a focus on promoting healing, resilience, and social change.

See, I came from parents who experienced childhood trauma too. When my paternal grandmother passed away, my father was 16 years old. Now when I was 16, I remember having to help plan a funeral for one of my friends that lost her mother. To help plan a funeral, be there for my friend for moral support, do my homework and be home before my 10 pm curfew with no car was a lot, but I did it because I did not want my friend to have to go through that experience alone. I did not know at the time that most of my friends were becoming cycle breakers like me. A cycle breaker is someone who sees an unhealthy cycle of behavior in their family and works to annihilate that cycle. As an adolescent, I carried the generational trauma of my parents around with me like I carried my heavy backpack going to school. For those like me, we all did! My parents' childhood trauma did not allow them to even finish high school. My dad enlisted as a U.S. Marine at the age of 16 (before the law was changed to 18) and my mom had my oldest brother when she was 16 years old. Depending on the situation, I would go home and have to endure different types of household challenges (I will go into details about later) and those household challenges had a major impact on me. I had to wake up the next day and transform back into a student all over again, which included carrying my own backpack of burdens that I was experiencing growing up as an adolescent pretty much everyday. I repeated this cycle often until I was able to learn and gather a better understanding of what those experiences were.

My parents, shaped by their personal childhood experiences, carried the weight of trauma, forming a narrative defined by shared pain and the resilience that emerged from it. In my family's long history, there's a theme that keeps coming up in our stories. It's all about loss. Both my parents went through loss, even though we grew up in different times. My dad lost his mother, my mother lost her mother, and I never got the chance to meet my paternal grandmother.

My father was only 16 years old when his beloved mother, my paternal grandmother, passed away unexpectedly. My paternal grandfather embarked on a series of three marriages, each bringing new dynamics and relationships into our family circle. As the years went by, the pain of that loss never truly faded, but it was woven into the fabric of my father's life, becoming a part of his story and a part of mine. He often shared stories of his mother, her kindness, her wisdom, and her unwavering love. Through his memories, she became a living presence in my childhood, a figure who was both absent and ever-present.

Since my dad was just a teenager when his mom died, he was way too young to deal with something so heavy. The pain of losing her hit him very hard, leaving a big hole in his life that no one could seem to fill. It changed everything for him. In the face of such heartbreak, my father made a life-changing decision—he enlisted in the military at the earliest opportunity. It was like he was looking for comfort in the organized and disciplined army lifestyle. He wanted to get away from all the sadness and find some meaning in life. His departure added another layer of absence to our family, but it also ignited a spark of resilience and strength within him. His time in the military shaped him into a man of character and integrity, qualities that he later passed on to his children and grandchildren. Through his service, he found a new family among his fellow soldiers, forging bonds that would last a lifetime. Yet, even as he embraced his new life, the memories of his mother remained firmly etched in his heart.

The loss of my paternal grandmother not only left a profound impact on my father but also resonated through generations. Growing up, the absence of my grandmother was a constant reminder of how precious life is and how love lasts forever. Her love for our family went beyond time and space, leaving a mark on our hearts even though none of us ever got the chance to meet her. Through stories and photographs, we pieced together fragments of her life, creating a tapestry of memories that connected us to her. We learned about her kindness, her sense of humor, and her unwavering strength in the face of adversity. Her spirit lived on through us, guiding our actions and inspiring us to cherish every moment with the people we love. When my paternal grandma suddenly passed away, it left a lasting impact on our entire family, creating a mix of sadness, love, and memories. It showed us that even in times of great sorrow, the love we share can last forever. Her absence left a void, but it also ignited a fire within us, a determination to live our lives to the fullest and honor her memory.

My mother's past unfolded like an alternate narrative. Picture my mom's childhood like this crazy quilt of experiences. Her mom, who you'd think should've been this constant source of love and comfort, turned out to be this mix of ChatGPT unpredictable emotions and erratic behaviors, stemming from her own unresolved traumas and challenges. There were periods of both abuse and neglect, leaving my mother navigating an emotional roller coaster growing up. This assortment of experiences shaped her resilience and resourcefulness, but it also left behind threads of uncertainty and longing for stability that she carried into adulthood.

Like, in a perfect world, your mom is supposed to be your rock, right? A solid support system to help you deal with all the growing-up stuff. But in my mom's case, that warm and nurturing mom-vibe was overshadowed by this weird feeling of her being there, but not really. I found out when I was a teenager that she actually existed and had a whole family that lived eight hours from us in Chicago when we resided in Kansas City, Mo.

It wasn't just a physical absence for my mom either; it was this emotional gap that took over her growing-up years. Even though her mom was miles away physically, this emotional disconnect left this big hole where there should've been all this motherly advice, understanding, and love. And that missing emotional link messed with my mom's sense of security and how she saw relationships. Imagine my mom's childhood as this balancing act – she wanted the emotional support a mom should give, but it was like trying to grab onto something that kept slipping away. This confusing dance with her mom had a lasting impact and shaped how she sees love, trust, and connection. The absence of her mom's physical and emotional presence became a major part of her early years, influencing how she dealt with feelings and the relationships she got into later on.

Basically, thinking about her mom as this important but kind of distant figure highlights how family relationships can get very complicated. It's a reminder of how a parent's emotional availability, or lack of it, can seriously mess with a kid's development and how they understand love and feeling secure. Life's complicated, huh? This abandonment carved a deep and lasting wound within her young heart, leaving an imprint that would shape her life. Not having her mom around left a deep scar that never really went away. It was like a never-ending reminder of all the love that was missing in her life. It became a part of her story, a chapter that had shaped her into the person she had become. As a toddler, my mother yearned for the comfort and reassurance that only a mother's embrace could provide. But fate had other plans, and she was left to navigate the world without her primary source of unconditional love.

In the story of my mother's childhood, joy, laughter, and the warmth of familial bonds did exist. Raised by her grandmother and father, she was surrounded by love and care. However, embedded deep within her heart was a void that could not be filled, a silent ache that whispered in the shadows of her memories. As a kid, she kept feeling that her mom didn't want her, like she was always alone, and it just wouldn't go away. It was like a dark cloud hanging over her childhood. On the other hand, my maternal grandfather's astonishing eight remarriages created a dynamic family land-scape filled with numerous step-siblings and half-siblings for my mother. The confused nature of my maternal grandfather's multiple marriages created an unstable and chaotic family environment, characterized by emo-tional turmoil and interpersonal conflict amongst his children. As a result, my mother struggled to navigate the challenges of adolescence, ultimately becoming a teenage mother at the age of 16. Growing up, I had a bunch of cousins, which was cool. But my mom was going through some tough stuff, which made things at home really hard for her.

My parents' and grandparents' lives have taught me a lot about what it means to be human and how important family is, even when things get tough. Growing up, I was surrounded by a bunch of cousins. It was like having a built-in squad to hang out with. We went to school together, and it always felt like we had each other's backs. As my family grew through marriages, my network of cousins kept expanding. It was like meeting a whole new bunch of friends, each with their own unique personalities and perspectives. My friends and I used to joke about it, but it was my truth!

My family serves as an educational example of generational trauma—a term that captures the enduring impact of traumatic events from decades past on the understanding, coping mechanisms, and healing processes of subsequent generations. The absence of mothers in my parents' lives was a trauma in itself, a theme that would resonate through my own experiences. Generational trauma is like this long-lasting family vibe that gets passed down, you know? It's not just about the crazy stories or the drama; it's this invisible force shaping our lives. Take my parents, for example. Dad faced some serious stuff when he was just 16, and Mom had her share of rough times as a teen too. Their struggles have left an indelible mark, creating a kind of family history that goes beyond the usual family tree.

So, now you know too! I've got this secret baggage of pain and tough times that were sneakily handed down through the generations. It's not like it comes with a manual or anything, but it's there, shaping the story of my life. I've realized I didn't just inherit their eye color or laugh; I got this whole narrative of resilience and survival, plus all the ways they figured out how to cope with their own tough times.

This family legacy explains a lot about the challenges I've faced. It's like a behind-the-scenes look at my life showing me the struggles, patterns, and ways I've learned to deal with stuff. The transfer of this generational baggage has made for this mix of feelings, behaviors, and coping strategies that make up who I am. Understanding how generational trauma works has given me a new lens to look at my own story. It's not just about my personal struggles – they're part of a bigger picture, connected to my family's history. My life story is like a mix of personal experiences and this family legacy that goes way back. Recognizing and dealing with the impact of generational trauma lets me carve out a path towards healing, resilience, and breaking free from the stuff that's been tying my family down. My parents' stories echo in my heart and mind, shaping how I see the world and how I react to things. It's made me realize that I need to take a deep dive into myself, to figure out who I am and how I can break free from the cycle of pain that seems to keep repeating.

When I really started to look at myself, I saw how my family's history has affected me in ways I never noticed before. There are certain behaviors I do, emotions I feel, and beliefs I hold that I realized were passed down from generation to generation. It's been eye-opening and overwhelming to see how much of my past is still with me. However, amidst the shadows cast by intergenerational trauma, I have also discovered a wellspring of resilience and hope. Through the practice of compassion towards myself and others, I have begun to cultivate an inner sanctuary of healing and transformation.

I have learned to embrace my flaws and imperfections, recognizing them as part of my human experience. Knowing this doesn't just help me make sense of things; it also pushes me to break the cycle. I want to heal, not just for myself, but to stop passing down this invisible weight to the next generation.

My parents made choices that weren't always easy and left our sibling squad with a bunch of challenges during our teenage years. Things at home were rough. The drama didn't stop at the front door though—school was extremely hard for us. We had to deal with family drama, schoolwork, and the pressure to get good grades even when our personal lives were a total mess. Every school day was like a rollercoaster ride of challenges that mirrored the chaos we faced at home. The pressure to succeed in school, fit in socially, and deal with unresolved family issues was like a never-ending battle. It felt like the walls of our classrooms couldn't protect us from the emotional storms brewing in our homes. The things we learned in textbooks coupled with the challenges we were dealing with at home, created a wild mix of experiences that shaped who we are today.

Coping with family issues while trying to maintain academic excellence was a continuous balancing act. The weight of our family's problems pressed down upon us, casting a heavy shadow over our ability to focus and concentrate in class. The emotional turmoil we carried with us from home invaded our study sessions making it difficult to absorb and retain information. Sleep eluded us, replaced by anxious thoughts and worries about our family's well-being. The mental and emotional exhaustion we endured made it challenging to perform well academically.

The challenges of our adolescence taught us valuable lessons about life, adversity, and the importance of resilience. We learned that life is not always fair, that it presents us with obstacles that can either break us or make us stronger. We discovered the significance of seeking support from others, finding strength in our relationships, and relying on the kindness and compassion of those who care about us. The hardships we faced as children have shaped us into the adults we are today, equipping us with the tools necessary to navigate the complexities of life with greater understanding and empathy.

Growing up in the shadow of our parents' struggles, my friends and I found ourselves grappling with a mirror image of their pain. We all had ACEs, but childhood trauma did not officially have a name at that time. Unbeknownst to us, we were all silently carrying the weight of Adverse Childhood Experiences. This invisible burden, left unnamed and unrecognized, shaped our lives in profound ways.

Back then, we hadn't heard of the term "Adverse Childhood Experiences," but the impact of the difficult things we went through as kids left a lasting impression on us. From the emotional scars of neglect and abuse to the insidious whispers of poverty and addiction, our young hearts bore witness to a harsh reality. Our homes were supposed to be sanctuaries, but for many of us, they were anything but. Instead, they were battlefields where unspoken wounds festered and invisible wars raged. We learned to navigate a world of chaos and fear, developing survival mechanisms that would stay with us long after childhood.

The weight of ACEs manifested itself in various ways. Some of us struggled with behavioral issues, acting out in rebellion against the pain we couldn't articulate. Others retreated into themselves, becoming withdrawn and isolated. The scars of trauma were like ghosts that haunted our waking hours and tormented our dreams. Despite the darkness that surrounded us, there were glimmers of hope. In the midst of adversity, we found solace in our friendships. We understood each other's pain, and together, we created a makeshift family, a sanctuary where we could find acceptance and belonging. We drew strength from our shared experiences, forming a tight-knit group of friends who understood and supported one another.

It was during high school that I formed some of my most enduring friendships through extracurricular activities. I sang in Several We shared our joys and sorrows, our triumphs and failures. We laughed together, cried together, and grew together. We learned the true meaning of loyalty, compassion, and support. It was a time of intense emotions, both positive and negative.

Looking back, I realized that high school was more than just a stepping stone on the path to adulthood. It was a time of profound growth, self-discovery, and transformation. Many of my friends, also burdened by worries beyond the classroom, faced attendance issues, discipline problems, and, in extreme cases, dropped out of school. The stories of my friends, layered with adversity and household challenges, mirrored my own struggles. In the crazy quilt of my life, my friends and I have a lot of stuff we've been through together. As I hung out with my friends, I got to see all the ups and downs in their lives which were similar to what I was going through. It was like a rollercoaster ride of emotions! I saw how tough my friends could be, even when things got tough. Their stories totally resonated with me and made me think about my own life and all the stuff I've been through. It was like we were all in it together, like a big support group. We totally understood each other, and it was a safe space where we could be ourselves and dream big.

Through acts of compassion, encouragement, and guidance, I endeavored to be a source of strength for my friends. I listened, empathized, and offered a shoulder to lean on. I helped them navigate difficult decisions, provided practical advice, and celebrated their successes. We were breaking generational curses together. As I witnessed the positive impact we were having on others, having my own sense of purpose grew stronger. It was a transformative experience for both my friends and me. Together, we broke the chains of adversity and embarked on a path towards a brighter future. I am eternally grateful for the opportunity to have played a role in their lives and to have discovered my own purpose in the process. It is a testament to the interconnectedness of our experiences and the power of human connection to create positive change in the world.

Growing up with childhood trauma and sharing those experiences highlights the tough times, the obstacles, and the struggles I went through. I knew that my friends faced the same struggles too. We were definitely there for each other. It was like our lives were singing the same tune, but each of us had our own unique voice that made it special and created our own bonds. We had our own ups and downs, our dreams and our fears, but we're all in this thing called life together, and that's what made it so special. I discovered a reservoir of strength and resilience within myself that I never knew I possessed. I realized that my own struggles had equipped me with the tools and empathy necessary to guide others through their own challenges.

Knowledge of ACEs is instrumental in preventing adverse outcomes associated with childhood trauma. By addressing the root causes, individuals and communities can implement preventive measures, reducing the likelihood of negative health, social, and behavioral outcomes.

CHAPTER 5

PREVENTING ADVERSE OUTCOMES

The concept of Adverse Childhood Experiences (ACEs) has gained attention in recent years, but it is surprising that many people remain unaware of its significance. It is not uncommon for individuals to be unfamiliar with the term "ACEs" and its profound impact on children's lives for several reasons:

1. **Lack of Awareness**: Many people have not been exposed to information about ACEs in their personal or professional lives. Awareness of ACEs and their impact may be limited in certain communities, educational settings, or professional circles.

2. **Stigma and Taboo**: Discussions about childhood trauma and adversity can be stigmatized or considered taboo in some cultural or social contexts. As a result, individuals may avoid or dismiss conversations about ACEs, leading to a lack of understanding about their significance.

3. **Limited Education and Training**: Professionals in various fields, including education, healthcare, and social services, may not have received adequate education or training on ACEs and trauma-informed care. Without this foundational knowledge, individuals

may not fully grasp the importance of addressing ACEs in their work or personal lives.

4. **Misconceptions and Misunderstandings**: There may be misconceptions or misunderstandings about ACEs and their implications. Some individuals may mistakenly believe that childhood adversity has minimal long-term effects or may not recognize the full extent of its impact on children's physical, emotional, and social well-being.

5. **Lack of Public Discourse:** ACEs have only recently gained attention as a public health issue, and discussions about childhood trauma may not have reached widespread audiences. Limited public discourse on ACEs may contribute to a lack of awareness among individuals who have not been directly exposed to this information.

Overall, addressing the gap in awareness and understanding of ACEs requires ongoing education, advocacy, and public awareness efforts to ensure that individuals recognize the profound impact of childhood adversity and the importance of trauma-informed approaches in supporting children's health and well-being.

Even among those who are aware of ACEs, there is often a reluctance to discuss the topic openly. This reluctance can be attributed to several factors. First, our society has inadvertently normalized ACEs. The prevalence of childhood trauma across different socioeconomic backgrounds and cultures has created a perception that these experiences are a common part of growing up. This normalization can lead to a sense of resignation and discourage individuals from seeking help or acknowledging the long-term effects of ACEs. Second, discussing ACEs can be emotionally challenging and triggering. Childhood trauma often involves sensitive and painful memories, making it difficult for individuals to share their experiences. Fear of judgment, stigma, or shame can also contribute to the reluctance to talk about ACEs.

Over two decades of research nationally and internationally illuminated a strong link between the number of ACEs experienced in childhood and the likelihood of physical and mental health issues persisting into adulthood, perpetuating a cycle that spans generations. The interconnectedness of our experiences is a profound aspect of human existence. It highlights how our interactions with others, our environment, and the world at large have a significant impact on shaping our lives. It is through these connections that we learn, grow, and create lasting memories. More importantly, it is through these connections that we have the power to create positive change in the world.

Addressing the lack of awareness and encouraging open conversations about ACEs is crucial for breaking down the barriers that prevent individuals from seeking support and healing. By raising awareness and creating a safe and supportive environment, we can empower individuals to confront their experiences, promote resilience, and ultimately mitigate the long-term consequences of ACEs. It will be tough to make these trauma-informed practices a reality in big systems and organizations with our educating and understanding. If we do not address ACEs, those who have experienced ACEs may suffer long-term consequences that will affect their health and well-being.

Background of the ACEs Study

In 1980, Dr. Vincent Felitti was the chief doctor at Kaiser Permanente's Preventive Medicine Department in San Diego, California. Felitti owned an obesity clinic that was designed for people who were 100 to 600 pounds overweight. Every year for five consecutive years, half the people in the obesity clinic dropped out. In 1985, Felitti realized that his clinic had a real and serious problem. After reviewing the dropouts' medical records, the data revealed that they were born at normal weight; however, their weight gain was anything but normal. Felitti decided to conduct face-to-face interviews with hundreds of the dropouts; he used standard sets of questions for everyone he interviewed. He posed several questions to the patients in the obesity program: "How much did you weigh when you were born?" "How old were you when you became sexually active?" It was not until he asked, "How much did you weigh when you were sexually active?" that Felitti realized that the patient was providing information about incest and childhood abuse.

Still shocked about his revelation, Felitti asked five colleagues to interview the next 100 patients in the weight program. His colleagues had the same revelations. Of the 286 people who Felitti and his colleagues interviewed, most had been sexually abused as a child. One patient who was raped when she was 23 years old gained 105 pounds in the year after she was attacked. Felitti realized that the obese patients did not see weight as the problem. Eating was the solution to make them feel better. Eating helped with anxiety, fear, and even depression. For other patients, being obese solved the problem. As a result, losing weight brought back those fears. Felitti did not realize at that time that he would provide an understanding to millions of people who use coping methods to deal with depression, fear, and anger. He shared with his patients what he had learned from evaluating the charts. Some patients sent letters of thanks because of the new program that he created.

In 1990, Felitti presented his results from the clinic, but his insights were not well received. However, Dr. David Williamson, an epidemiologist from the CDC was intrigued by the study. Felitti and Williamson met with a group of researchers that included Dr. Robert Anda. Anda was engaged in a study on depression and coronary heart disease when he was chosen to join the team with Felitti and Williamson. The doctors spent more than a year researching literature on childhood trauma. In 1995, the distribution of ACEs surveys began.

The original ACEs study was conducted in 1995 from the Kaiser Permanente's Appraisal Clinic in San Diego, California, which is one of the nation's largest medical evaluation centers. Kaiser Permanente was chosen as the center of choice because more than 50,000 members came through the preventative medicine department each year. A little more than 13,000 members completed a standardized medical evaluation at the clinic between August and November 1995 and January and March 1996. A second mailing was sent from the clinic to people who did not respond initially. An additional 9,500 participants completed the survey through the mail. All of the ACEs questions in the questionnaire refer to the participant's first 18 years of life. Figure 1 shows ACEs and the pyramid influence on health, which can result in an early death.

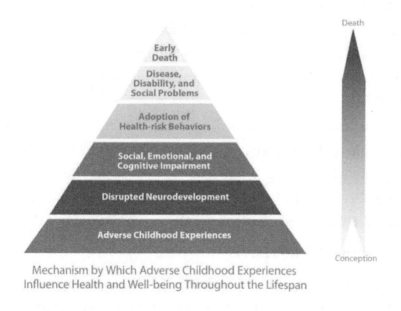

Mechanism by Which Adverse Childhood Experiences
Influence Health and Well-being Throughout the Lifespan

Figure 1. The adverse childhood experiences (ACES) pyramid represents the conceptual framework for the ACES Study. From "About the CDC-Kaiser ACE study" by Center for Disease Control and Prevention, 2016b, retrieved from http://www.cdc.gov/violenceprevention/acestudy/about.html Reprinted with permission.

The ACES study was conducted to determine the relationship between childhood experiences and its link to health problems. Childhood trauma can be significant in life. It can also have an impact across generations. Some of these experiences will have repercussions, which can permanently change your life.

Since 1995, numerous studies and research initiatives have been conducted globally to further explore the relationship between childhood adversity and various health, social, and behavioral outcomes. The field of ACEs research has expanded considerably, with ongoing studies investigating the prevalence, consequences, and potential interventions related to ACEs. Over the past several decades, the field of research and advocacy surrounding ACEs has witnessed remarkable growth and momentum on a global scale. This collective endeavor has facilitated a remarkable expansion of knowledge and understanding regarding the prevalence, impact, and potential consequences of ACEs.

The more I conducted research, the more I realized that our childhood relationships and experiences can affect our health and well-being. ACEs are very common! According to data collected from adults across all 50 states between 2011 and 2019, 64% reported experiencing at least ONE type of ACE and 17% reported experiencing FOUR or more types of ACEs.2

Dr. Nadine Burke Harris

Dr. Nadine Burke Harris's TED Talk in 2015 also served as a powerful catalyst for profound self-reflection and a deeper understanding of the intricacies of my own experiences. Her articulate presentation not only resonated with my journey but also provided a language—a vocabulary that was previously absent—to express the impact of my early experiences. In her words, I found a mirror reflecting the complexities of navigating childhood

---

2 - http://cdc.gov

trauma, a mirror that granted validation to emotions and struggles that had long been unspoken.

The TED Talk became a pivotal moment of recognition. This revelation was transformative, as it allowed me to contextualize my own journey within a broader framework of understanding. Dr. Burke Harris's work served as a beacon, illuminating a path through the complexities of trauma and offering insights into resilience and healing. It also added a wealth of updated research on behalf of ACEs.

As an inspiration, Dr. Burke Harris embodies the transformative power of turning adversity into advocacy. Her commitment to raising awareness about ACEs, coupled with her dedication to fostering a culture of resilience and compassion, resonates deeply with my own aspirations. Her work goes beyond shedding light on the challenges; it is a call to action, an invitation to advocate for change and contribute to a collective understanding of the profound effects of early experiences on individuals and communities.

Furthermore, Dr. Burke Harris's mentorship, albeit indirect, lies in the wisdom imparted through her insights and the guidance found in her work. The acknowledgment of her influence is a recognition of the impact she has had on shaping my perspectives, fostering empathy, and encouraging a commitment to breaking generational cycles.

In essence, acknowledging Dr. Nadine Burke Harris as my inspiration and mentor is an acknowledgment of gratitude for the invaluable insights she has provided and the transformative role she has played in my journey of self-discovery and healing. It is a tribute to her advocacy, which has not only empowered me to navigate my own experiences but has also inspired a commitment to advocate for others facing similar challenges.

Understanding ACEs contributes to the creation of a supportive environment. Communities that are aware of the prevalence of childhood trauma can develop resources, programs, and support networks to help individuals and families cope, heal, and thrive.

CHAPTER 6

CREATING A SUPPORTING ENVIRONMENT

I realized that addressing the challenges faced by students requires an approach that involves collaboration among schools, families and communities. Schools will need to create supportive learning environments that are responsive to students' needs. This includes providing access to mental health services, academic support, and extracurricular activities that promote positive youth development. Families play a primary role in providing a stable and nurturing home environment, which includes involvement in their children's education. Communities need to offer safe and enriching environments for young people, with opportunities for recreation, mentorship, and skill-building. Schools, families, and communities all play a vital role in addressing the challenges faced by students. A comprehensive approach that involves collaboration among these three groups is essential to creating supportive learning environments and promoting positive youth development.

Schools:

- **Create supportive learning environments** that are responsive to students' needs as this is essential for their academic success and overall well-being. This includes providing a safe and welcoming atmosphere, access to mental health services, academic support, and extracurricular activities that promote positive youth development.

Safe and Welcoming Atmosphere:

- Establish a culture of respect, empathy, and inclusion where students feel safe and respected.
- Promote diversity and inclusivity by celebrating different cultures, identities, and perspectives.
- Ensure that all students have a sense of belonging and feel connected to the school community.
- Implement anti-bullying policies and programs to create a safe environment for all students.

Access to Mental Health Services:

- Provide students with access to mental health professionals such as counselors, psychologists, and social workers.
- Promote mental health awareness and reduce stigma by educating students and staff about mental health issues.
- Offer confidential counseling services to students who need support and guidance.
- Develop partnerships with community mental health organizations to ensure continuity of care.

Academic Support:

- Offer individualized academic support to students who are struggling or need additional assistance.
- Provide tutoring services, study groups, and after-school programs to help students succeed academically.

- Create a supportive classroom environment where students feel comfortable asking questions and seeking help.
- Promote a growth mindset by encouraging students to embrace challenges and learn from their mistakes.

Extracurricular Activities:

- Offer a variety of extracurricular activities that cater to different interests and talents.
- Encourage students to participate in extracurricular activities as they provide opportunities for socialization, skill development, and leadership.
- Ensure that extracurricular activities are inclusive and accessible to all students, regardless of their abilities or socioeconomic status.
- Recognize and celebrate students' achievements in extracurricular activities.

It is important for those students who can be identified with ACES to get involved with extracurricular activities (EA). Extracurricular activities provide opportunities for cultivating interests and talents, introducing and developing interpersonal and life skills, gaining insight into competencies and passions, and broadening social, capital connections with peers and significant adults. Used as a tool, EA can promote relationships and environments that help children grow up to be healthy and productive citizens; EA can be used to help build stronger and safer families and communities for all children involved.

Addressing ACEs fosters resilience on an individual and community level. Through education, support, and intervention, individuals can develop the skills and coping mechanisms needed to overcome the effects of childhood trauma, contributing to the resilience of the entire community.

CHAPTER 7

BUILDING RESILIENT COMMUNITIES

What is Extracurricular Activity? (EA)

EA are activities that students enjoy a sense of freedom without academic struggles. EA includes interscholastic sports, fine arts, academic clubs, student councils, honor societies, cheerleading, and dance. The term EA comes from Joseph Lee, known as the "Father of the Playground Movement," who suggested that play is essential to moral and human development. Lee believed when a child is nurtured in a spirit of recreation, the instincts will harmonize, and the end result will be the morally mature individual.

The history of EA can be traced to the early 1910s. The book, *The Twenty-fifth Yearbook of the National Society for the Study of Education* was dedicated as a study of EA in the school. The numerous authors included in the book ignited several books that highlighted research for support of EA. The development of EA was slow in the beginning, with many seeing it simply as a fad that would pass and quickly fade out of style. Historical participation in activities has led to an increase in academic skills, student achievement, appropriate student behaviors, and attendance. Activities are offered at every level within the school setting; therefore, opportunities are numerous for students to become involved. They provide a sense of freedom from the pressures of schoolwork and allow students to explore their interests and develop their skills. EAs can be anything from sports to clubs to student government, and they are found in schools all over the world.

There are numerous opportunities for students to actively participate in EA, which play a crucial role in their overall development. Schools typically provide a range of EAs at every level, encompassing elementary school to high school, catering to the diverse interests and passions of students. These activities extend beyond the classroom, offering valuable learning experiences and enabling students to explore their talents, build essential skills, and foster personal growth.

In elementary school, extracurricular activities (EAs) play a vital role in fostering students' overall development beyond academics. EAs primarily concentrate on honing foundational skills while nurturing creativity and allowing students to explore their interests. Common examples of EAs at the elementary level include art clubs, where children engage in various art forms such as painting, drawing, and sculpture, developing their artistic abilities and self-expression. Music ensembles provide an opportunity for students to learn instruments, sing in choirs, or participate in the band, fostering teamwork, rhythm, and musical appreciation. Sports teams, including basketball, soccer, and track and field, promote physical fitness, teamwork, and sportsmanship. Creative and performing arts EAs, such as theater productions, dance troupes, and choirs, allow students to express themselves artistically and develop their talents. Specifically, drama clubs encourage students to express themselves creatively through theater, enhancing their communication, collaboration, and public speaking skills.

As students progress to middle school and high school, the range of EAs expands significantly. In addition to the aforementioned elementary school activities, middle school and high school students have access to a broader spectrum of academic and non-academic EAs. Academic clubs, such as math clubs, provide a platform for students with a passion for mathematics to explore advanced concepts, engage in problem-solving competitions, and participate in math-related activities. Science clubs allow students to delve deeper into scientific subjects, conduct experiments, and learn about the latest scientific advancements. Debate teams foster critical thinking, research, and public speaking skills as students engage in formal debates on various topics.

Beyond academic clubs, there are numerous non-academic EAs that cater to diverse interests and talents. These include language clubs, which focus on learning and practicing foreign languages, promoting cultural awareness and global citizenship. Student government and leadership clubs provide opportunities for students to develop leadership skills, decision-making abilities, and a sense of responsibility. Community service EAs, such as volunteering at local organizations or participating in environmental projects, instill a sense of social responsibility and provide students with a platform to make a positive impact on their surroundings. Yearbook and newspaper clubs allow students to showcase their writing, photography, and design skills while documenting school events and capturing memories.

Overall, the availability of a wide range of extracurricular activities in elementary school, middle school, and high school enriches students' educational experience. EAs provide avenues for students to pursue their interests, develop their talents, learn new skills, and make meaningful connections with peers and mentors. They also contribute to students' overall personal growth and development, preparing them to become well-rounded individuals ready to embrace the challenges and opportunities of the future.

In addition to school-based EAs, students can also find opportunities in their community. Public libraries often offer EAs related to reading, writing, and technology. Community centers and recreation centers may have sports leagues, dance classes, and arts and crafts programs. Local museums, theaters, and historical societies frequently organize educational programs and workshops. Overall, the involvement in extracurricular activities offers students a well-rounded education, preparing them for success in college, career, and life. By embracing the diverse opportunities available, students can enrich their educational experience, cultivate their interests, and become well-rounded individuals.

Extracurricular activities can help students to develop important life skills, such as time management, responsibility, and cooperation. In addition to extrinsic rewards, such as college admission or scholarships, these rewards can include a sense of accomplishment, self-confidence, and belonging. Participation in EAs can provide students with a sense of purpose and direction, as they work towards achieving their goals and contributing to their community. Furthermore, EAs can help students to develop a strong work ethic, learn how to manage their time effectively, and build their leadership skills.

Consequently, students who actively participate in EAs often demonstrate higher levels of academic achievement and a deeper understanding of the subject matter. In addition to boosting self-esteem and academic performance, the sense of accomplishment derived from EAs also contributes to the development of important life skills. As students navigate the challenges and successes of their experiences, they learn valuable lessons about perseverance, resilience, and problem-solving. They develop the ability to adapt to changing circumstances, manage their time effectively, and work collaboratively with others. These skills are essential for success not only in school but also in the workplace and in life in general. By providing students with opportunities to engage in meaningful and engaging activities, educators can help them unlock the transformative potential of this profound reward.

If you haven't noticed, extracurricular activity is everything to me. Participation in extracurricular activities saved my life! You can participate in EA at every level within the school setting. From elementary school to the college experience, opportunities are numerous for students to become involved. EA can play a meaningful role in the life of a student. The desire to participate in EA can play a strong role in encouraging students to attend school and engage in class. Participation in EA can be designed to increase student engagement and motivation for school, which includes positive relations with their peers as well as adults.

I stayed involved in EC throughout my high school journey by participating in EC in school, singing in several choirs in my community and as a member of the Boys and Girls Club. I also wrote for Hallmark Cards and performed with the Marching Cobras around the globe. My EC list is pretty extensive! I stayed involved in some type of activity until the summer before I left to attend Central Missouri State University known today as the University of Central Missouri. I got involved in EC as soon as I got to CMSU/UCM with my best friend who was also my roommate. We both joined the black governing organization freshman year known as the Association of Black Collegiates (ABC). I got into the choir (ABCGC) and my best friend got into dance (ABCDC). We became popular as freshmen very quickly. Those activities provided us with opportunities to connect with others who shared similar passions, further strengthening their sense of community and belonging.

Overall, the sense of belonging fostered in EAs can be a powerful driver of student success. It contributes to students' well-being, motivation, and academic achievement by providing a supportive environment where students feel connected, valued, and empowered. EAs can equip students with the essential tools to thrive in life and pursue their goals with confidence. Furthermore, EAs can provide students with a sense of purpose and direction. By setting goals, working towards achieving them, and contributing to their community through EAs, students can develop a sense of meaning and purpose in their lives. This sense of purpose helps them stay motivated and focused on their long-term aspirations.

The feeling of accomplishment that comes from being involved in an EA can be a powerful motivator for students. When students work hard and see their efforts pay off, it can give them a sense of pride and satisfaction. This sense of accomplishment can carry over into other areas of their lives, such as their academic work and personal relationships.

Self-confidence is another important intrinsic reward that students can gain from participating in EAs. When students are involved in activities that they enjoy and are good at, it can help to boost their self-esteem. This can lead to students feeling more confident in their abilities and more willing to take on new challenges.

Belonging is a fundamental human need, and EAs can provide students with a sense of belonging to a community. When students are involved in EAs, they are surrounded by other students who share their interests and goals. This can help students to feel connected to others and to develop a sense of identity.

In addition to the intrinsic rewards mentioned above, EAs can also help students to make new friends, learn new skills, and develop their interests. EAs provide students with opportunities to interact with other students who share their interests, which can lead to the development of new friendships. Students can also learn new skills, such as leadership, teamwork, and communication, through their involvement in EAs. Finally, EAs can help students to develop their interests and explore new areas of study.

In the end, feeling like you belong in an EA is imperative.. It helps students feel good about themselves, do well in school, and feel like their life has meaning. When EAs are supportive and make students feel like they're part of something, it can really help them grow as people and find their way in the world. The sense of belonging cultivated in EAs stems from various factors. Small class sizes and close-knit communities create a sense of intimacy and familiarity among students and faculty. Students feel known and understood, which contributes to their sense of security and belonging. If it was not for participation in EA, I do not know where I would be today.

To assist in the prevention of ACEs-related consequences in the adolescent years, participation in EA might be an essential key to the health and welfare of adolescents. If ACEs can be identified at an early age, there is a strong chance that ACEs-related health consequences could be prevented. To this date, there is no data that links ACEs with ongoing issues inside of the school such as attendance or discipline. However, my dissertation study provides the data needed to support the correlation between ACEs scores and EA. All of the current research is circumstantial. The results of the study can be useful not only to support students at school with ACES, but also to provide possible solutions to an on-going issue. ACEs are real-life situations that occur often. Once individuals who have endured ACEs are identified, solution data might be readily available for other students looking for help with their issues.

Knowledge about ACEs encourages the adoption of trauma-informed approaches in various settings, such as schools, workplaces, and healthcare. This involves recognizing the prevalence of trauma, responding with sensitivity, and creating environments that support healing and growth.

CHAPTER 8

PROMOTING TRAUMA-INFORMED APPROACHES

P romoting trauma-informed approaches is a crucial step in creating environments that are sensitive to the needs of individuals who have experienced trauma. It involves raising awareness, providing education, and implementing supportive practices that can help people heal and thrive. As I listened to my students over the years, I recognized the echoes of my own experiences in their voices. The same feelings of fear, shame, and isolation that had once consumed me were mirrored in their stories. This profound connection allowed me to empathize with them on a deeper level, creating a space where they felt seen, heard, and understood. Through these interactions, I realized that my experiences were not just my own but also shared by countless others, including my students. This revelation shattered the illusion of isolation and opened my eyes to the prevalence of childhood trauma. It became evident that addressing the impact of trauma was not just a personal endeavor but a societal imperative as well.

Armed with this newfound understanding, I committed myself to creating trauma-informed educational practices. I sought out training and resources, attended conferences, and engaged in professional development opportunities to deepen my knowledge and skills in supporting students who had experienced trauma. Incorporating trauma-informed principles into my teaching approach had a transformative impact on my classroom. I became more mindful of how my words and actions could potentially trigger students' trauma responses. I created a safe and supportive environment where students felt comfortable sharing their feelings and experiences. By fostering a trauma-informed classroom culture, I observed positive changes in my students. They became more engaged in their learning, demonstrated improved self-regulation skills, and developed stronger relationships with their peers. Most importantly, they began to heal and thrive, finding the strength to overcome the challenges they faced.

Many individuals with ACEs may feel isolated or misunderstood due to the stigma surrounding trauma. Raising awareness and providing education about ACEs helps validate their experiences and fosters a better understanding of the challenges they face. When individuals feel heard and understood, it can promote healing and resilience.

Raising Awareness:

- **Public Awareness Campaigns:** Initiate public awareness campaigns to educate the community about trauma and its impact on individuals and society.
- **Media Representation:** Encourage accurate and sensitive portrayal of trauma in media to foster greater understanding and empathy.
- **Community Dialogues:** Organize community dialogues and events to facilitate open discussions and break the stigma associated with trauma.

Awareness and education initiatives can connect individuals with ACEs to valuable resources and support services. By understanding the impact of ACEs and the available avenues for support, individuals can access the help they need to address trauma-related issues, such as counseling, therapy, support groups, and community services. Education about ACEs can empower individuals to break the cycle of trauma within their families and communities. By understanding how childhood experiences can impact future health and well-being, individuals can make informed choices to create healthier environments for themselves and future generations.

***Providing Education*:**

- **Trauma-Informed Training:** Offer trauma-informed training for professionals working in healthcare, education, social services, and law enforcement.
- **Curriculum Integration:** Incorporate trauma-informed principles into educational curricula, starting from early childhood.
- **Online Resources:** Develop online resources, including webinars, articles, and videos, to educate the public and professionals about trauma.

Implementing trauma-informed practices in various settings, such as schools, workplaces, healthcare facilities, and community organizations can create supportive environments that promote healing and resilience. These practices involve recognizing the prevalence and impact of trauma, prioritizing safety and trust, and offering compassionate and empowering support. Education about ACEs can help individuals develop resilience by understanding how trauma affects the brain and behavior. By learning coping strategies and resilience-building techniques, individuals can develop the skills they need to navigate challenges, manage stress, and thrive despite past adversities. Raising awareness and implementing supportive practices contribute to the creation of communities that prioritize empathy, compassion, and understanding. By fostering a culture of support and acceptance, individuals with ACEs can feel more connected and empowered to seek help and support from those around them.

Implementing Supportive Practices:

- **Trauma-Sensitive Care:** Implement trauma-sensitive practices in healthcare settings, ensuring that care is provided in a way that minimizes retraumatization.

- **Trauma-Responsive Schools:** Create trauma-responsive schools that prioritize building safe and supportive environments for students.

- **Trauma-Informed Workplaces:** Foster trauma-informed workplaces that recognize the impact of trauma on employees and provide appropriate support.

- **Peer Support Networks:** Establish peer support networks where individuals who have experienced trauma can connect and share their experiences.

- **Trauma-Informed Policy Advocacy:** Advocate for trauma-informed policies at the local, state, and federal levels to ensure a comprehensive approach.

Overall, raising awareness, providing education, and implementing supportive practices create a foundation for healing and thriving for individuals with adverse childhood experiences. By addressing the impact of trauma and creating environments that prioritize safety, trust, and support, we can empower individuals to overcome challenges and lead fulfilling lives.

By implementing these strategies, we can create a society that is more informed, compassionate, and equipped to support individuals who have experienced trauma, empowering them to heal and live fulfilling lives:

1. Education and Training: Offer workshops, seminars, and training sessions to educate individuals and organizations about ACEs and trauma-informed care by providing information on the prevalence

and impact of ACEs, as well as strategies for creating safe and supportive environments.

2. <u>Integration into Policies and Practices</u>: Advocate for trauma-informed approaches to be integrated into policies and practices across various sectors, including education, healthcare, social services, and criminal justice. This may involve revising protocols, guidelines, and procedures to prioritize trauma-informed care.

3. <u>Building Supportive Environments</u>: Create environments that prioritize safety, trust, and empowerment. This can include establishing trauma-informed practices such as clear communication, respect for boundaries, and opportunities for self-expression and autonomy.

4. <u>Providing Resources and Support</u>: Ensure that individuals with ACEs have access to resources and support services, including mental health counseling, support groups, and peer mentoring programs. Connect individuals with community resources and organizations that specialize in trauma-informed care.

5. <u>Collaboration and Partnerships</u>: Collaborate with other organizations, agencies, and stakeholders to promote trauma-informed approaches and share best practices. Partner with schools, healthcare providers, community centers, and advocacy groups to create a network of support for individuals with ACEs.

6. <u>Empowering Individuals and Communities</u>: Empower individuals with ACEs to be active participants in their own healing process. Provide opportunities for them to share their experiences, voice their needs, and advocate for change within their communities.

7. <u>Addressing Stigma and Discrimination</u>: Challenge stigma and discrimination surrounding ACEs and mental health issues. Promote understanding, empathy, and acceptance, and work to reduce barriers to accessing care and support services.

Open discussions about ACEs help reduce the stigma and shame associated with childhood trauma. When individuals understand that they are not alone in their experiences, it can lead to a more open and supportive dialogue, breaking down barriers to seeking help.

CHAPTER 9

REDUCING STIGMA AND SHAME

E ven though ACEs involve significant health-related issues, it has not been addressed in schools. If there are ACEs-related issues that are occurring at school, then they need to be managed properly. Most students are referred to the social worker or their ACEs-related issues are allowed to manifest into disciplinary and attendance-related issues. Teachers do not have access to what occurs to students after they leave their classroom or to the issues that might occur to students while they are outside the school building. Too many school districts are without access to ACEs-related information needed to help minimize these issues. Some students commit crimes and get sent to juvenile detention; some students are set up for the school to prison pipeline; some students drop out of school.

Although there is no simple solution to ACES, the lack of understanding may be a factor. To date, some students carry those burdens with them daily. Many students have no one to discuss or share their ACEs with. They have to keep their issues to themselves. Some students are not aware that there are resources that they can use within their school. In some school districts, there are no positive interventions that support students with ACESs because most teachers are not aware that their students suffer with the residuals.

Through my dissertation research, I found that the cycle of trauma can be passed down from generation to generation. It occurred to me that my childhood experiences and the difficult times my parents faced as kids were all linked. It had been years since those early days when I was asking questions and was told to stay out of grown folks business. It took some serious personal soul-searching and educational research that helped me finally put it all together. Parental trauma, often stemming from ACEs can manifest in various ways, including inconsistent parenting, emotional neglect, or even abuse. Recognizing this intergenerational transmission of trauma allowed me to gain a deeper understanding of my parents' behaviors and the challenges they faced in raising me.

I realized that the effects of childhood trauma extend beyond the individual. It can have a ripple effect, shape family dynamics, relationships, and the overall trajectory of lives. My parents' childhood trauma had not only impacted their parenting but also influenced their communication patterns, conflict resolution strategies, and emotional expressiveness within our family. I also discovered a profound connection between my personal experiences of childhood trauma and the experiences shared by my students. The realization came as a startling revelation, a sudden flash of insight that illuminated the connections between my own life journey and the stories entrusted to me by my students. It was a moment of profound recognition. The common thread of pain, vulnerability, and resilience that ran through both of our experiences that was shared. This transformative moment not only deepened my empathy but also ignited a renewed sense of purpose in my role as the Director of Student Activities.

The weight of my responsibility shifted, expanding beyond the routine tasks and administrative duties of my position. I understood that my role transcended the boundaries of mere event planning and student engagement. It was through this realization that I embraced my role as a guide, a mentor, and a source of support for my students. Inspired by their resilience and the courage they demonstrated in sharing their stories, I became committed to creating an environment where they felt safe, valued, and empowered. I sought to foster a sense of community, where students could connect with one another, find their voices, and discover their strengths.

My journey as the Director of Student Activities became a testament to the power of empathy, connection, and resilience. Through my dedication to creating a supportive environment for my students, I had the privilege of witnessing countless transformations. I saw students overcome their challenges, embrace their vulnerabilities, and discover their inner strength. It was through their resilience and the shared experiences that we formed a bond that transcended the boundaries of a traditional student-faculty relationship.

With renewed dedication, I worked tirelessly to develop an innovative after-school program with initiatives that addressed the emotional, psychological, and academic needs of my students. I organized workshops on mindfulness with the Fashion Club, resilience building by having basketball tournaments, and stress management with Students Against Violence Everywhere (SAVE). I initiated peer mentorship programs where alumni provided guidance and support to their younger peers when they came back to visit.

By creating victory through understanding ACEs, individuals contribute to a collective healing process. Shared knowledge, support, and empathy create a community that acknowledges the impact of childhood trauma and actively works towards healing and positive change.

Contributing to Collective Healing

Contributing to collective healing can profoundly benefit individuals with Adverse Childhood Experiences (ACEs) through validation and empowerment, breaking the silence, building supportive networks, fostering empathy and understanding, advocacy for social change, and promoting resilience and well-being.

Validation and Empowerment: Sharing one's story and participating in collective healing efforts can validate the experiences of individuals with ACEs, helping them feel heard, understood, and empowered. By connecting with others who have similar experiences, individuals with ACEs can find a sense of belonging and solidarity, reducing feelings of isolation and shame.

My role as the Director of Student Activities was a journey of personal growth, empathy, and service that left an enduring impact on both my students and myself. I knew that despite their carefree attitudes, students had a lot going on inside – fears, dreams, and everything in between. I was lucky to be able to be there for them, to listen, and to let them know that I believed in them. I championed initiatives that fostered a culture of inclusivity, empathy, and self-care. I created spaces where students could connect with one another, share their experiences, and find comfort in the knowledge that they were not alone. My office also became a safe haven, where displaying true feelings wasn't seen as a sign of weakness. It was like a celebration of how strong and adaptable people can be. Growing up, I too grappled with the aftermath of traumatic events that left emotional scars on my young mind. The weight of these experiences often felt unbearable, casting a long shadow over my childhood. As I navigated the challenges of my own healing journey, I carried with me the desire to create a safe and supportive space for my students. Little did I know that my lived experiences would become an invaluable resource in my work as an educator. Over time, I found that students were drawn to me, sharing their own stories of trauma, loss, and adversity. Their willingness to confide in me spoke volumes about the trust and connection we had built.

Breaking the Silence: Collective healing efforts help break the silence surrounding ACEs and trauma, encouraging open and honest conversations about difficult topics. By speaking out and raising awareness, individuals with ACEs can challenge stigma and misinformation, creating a culture of empathy, understanding, and support. As I listened to my students over the years, I recognized the echoes of my own experiences in their voices. Through these interactions, I realized that my experiences were not just my own but also shared by countless others, including my students. This revelation shattered the illusion of isolation and opened my eyes to the prevalence of childhood trauma. It became evident that addressing the impact of trauma was not just a personal endeavor but a societal imperative as well.

Building Support Networks: Contributing to collective healing provides opportunities to build supportive relationships and networks with peers, advocates, and allies. These connections offer valuable emotional support, encouragement, and practical assistance, enhancing resilience and promoting healing. Armed with this newfound understanding from research and my doctoral studies, I committed myself to creating trauma-informed educational practices. I sought out training and resources, attended conferences, and engaged in professional development opportunities to deepen my knowledge and skills in supporting students who had experienced trauma. Incorporating trauma-informed principles into my teaching approach had a transformative impact on my classroom.

Fostering Empathy and Understanding: Collective healing efforts promote empathy, compassion, and understanding among individuals, communities, and society as a whole. By sharing stories, listening with empathy, and supporting one another, people develop a deeper understanding of the impact of ACEs and trauma, fostering a culture of empathy and solidarity. The realization of the shared experiences of childhood trauma between myself and my students was a turning point in my journey as an educator. It ignited a passion in me to create a more compassionate and trauma-sensitive educational system where all students can learn, grow, and reach their full potential. My experiences have taught me that education has the power to transform lives, and by embracing trauma-informed practices, we can create a brighter future for our children and generations to come.

Advocacy and Social Change: Contributing to collective healing empowers individuals to become advocates for change and champions for trauma-informed policies and practices. By sharing their experiences and advocating for systemic improvements, individuals with ACEs can help create more supportive and inclusive environments in schools, communities, healthcare settings, and beyond.

By creating supportive learning environments that address students' academic, emotional, and social needs, schools can help students thrive and reach their full potential. Training teachers and staff to be trauma-informed and culturally responsive with their own ACEs is a crucial step in promoting student well-being and academic success. By understanding their own ACEs, educators can develop empathy for their students who may have experienced similar or different forms of trauma.

Trauma-informed and culturally responsive practices involve creating a safe and supportive learning environment where students feel respected, valued, and understood. Educators who are trauma-informed can recognize the signs and symptoms of trauma in their students and respond in a way that is sensitive and supportive. They can also provide culturally responsive teaching that is tailored to the needs and experiences of their diverse students.

When teachers and staff are trauma-informed and culturally responsive, they are better able to:

- Build strong relationships with their students
- Create a safe and supportive learning environment
- Recognize and respond to the signs and symptoms of trauma
- Provide culturally responsive teaching
- Advocate for students who have experienced trauma
- Support students in developing resilience and coping skills

By investing in training for teachers and staff, schools can create a more positive and supportive learning environment for all students. This can lead to improved academic outcomes, reduced dropout rates, and increased social-emotional well-being for students. This will help them to understand the unique needs of students who have experienced trauma and to create a more inclusive learning environment. Training teachers and staff to be trauma-informed and culturally responsive is essential. Trauma-informed education recognizes that many students have experienced traumatic events in their lives, and it aims to address the impact of trauma on learning and behavior. Culturally responsive education acknowledges and respects the diverse cultural backgrounds of students and incorporates culturally relevant teaching practices.

When teachers and staff are trauma-informed, they are able to understand the unique needs of students who have experienced trauma. They are able to recognize the signs and symptoms of trauma, and they know how to respond in a way that is supportive and non-triggering. They are also able to create a classroom environment that is safe and welcoming for all students.

When teachers and staff are culturally responsive, they are able to create a learning environment that is inclusive of all students, regardless of their cultural background. They are able to incorporate culturally relevant materials and teaching practices into their lessons, and they are able to create a classroom environment that is welcoming and respectful of all cultures.

There are a number of benefits to training teachers and staff to be trauma-informed and culturally responsive. These benefits include:

- **Improved student outcomes.** Students who are taught by trauma-informed and culturally responsive teachers are more likely to succeed academically, have better attendance, and have fewer behavioral problems.
- **A more positive school climate.** Schools that have a trauma-informed and culturally responsive approach are more likely to have a positive school climate, which is characterized by safety, respect, and collaboration.
- **Increased parent engagement.** Parents are more likely to be engaged in their children's education when they feel that the school is a safe and welcoming place for their children.
- **Provide opportunities for students to develop social and emotional skills.** This can be done through social-emotional learning programs, mentoring programs, and other interventions. Providing opportunities for students to develop social and emotional skills is crucial for their overall well-being and success.

By integrating social-emotional learning (SEL) programs into the educational setting, students can acquire valuable skills such as self-awareness, self-management, social awareness, relationship skills, and responsible decision-making. These skills enable students to navigate social interactions, manage their emotions, build positive relationships, and make informed choices.

Promoting Resilience and Well-being: Participating in collective healing efforts can promote resilience, healing, and overall well-being for individuals with ACEs. By engaging in activities such as storytelling, art therapy, support groups, and community organizing, individuals can develop coping skills, strengthen their sense of identity and agency, and find meaning and purpose in their experiences.

Mentorship Programs

High school had its share of challenges and triumphs, but I fondly remember the opportunity to be a senior and take on the role of a mentor. Our freshman class that year was an incredible group, and taking some young ladies under my wing as a Big Sister was an incredibly rewarding experience. My goal was to ensure that they successfully made it through their freshman year without dropping out. Having witnessed so many of my friends succumb to dropping out, I was determined to help these young women avoid the same fate and experience the joy of graduation.

The decision to become a mentor stemmed from a deep desire to prevent them from enduring the same hardships that I had faced in high school. Graduating from high school was a significant milestone, especially considering that many of our parents had not had the same opportunity due to various circumstances. It was a privilege to be a part of their journey and to continue to stay in touch with them even after graduation.

Looking back, I realize that my passion for mentoring and supporting others stemmed from my own ACEs. Growing up in an environment marked by adversity has taught me the importance of resilience and empathy. By becoming a mentor, I hoped to provide the guidance and support that I had craved during my own difficult times.

Mentoring programs can also further enhance social and emotional development by pairing students with caring adults who serve as role models and provide guidance. Mentors can offer emotional support, help students develop coping mechanisms, and expose them to new experiences and opportunities. Mentoring programs play a pivotal role in fostering the social and emotional development of students by establishing meaningful relationships with caring adults who act as role models and offer guidance. These programs create a supportive environment that allows students to thrive and reach their full potential.

One of the primary benefits of mentoring programs is the provision of emotional support. Mentors listen actively, empathize, and validate students' feelings, creating a safe space for them to express themselves openly. By doing so, mentors help students develop a sense of self-worth, resilience, and emotional intelligence. They also help students identify and manage their emotions effectively, reducing the risk of developing mental health issues.

Mentors help students develop coping mechanisms to navigate the challenges and stressors they encounter in their daily lives. Mentors provide practical strategies for problem-solving, conflict resolution, and stress management. They also teach students how to cultivate inner strength, resilience, and a positive outlook, equipping them with the tools to overcome obstacles and setbacks. Mentors also play a crucial role in exposing students to new experiences and opportunities that they might not otherwise have access to. They may take students on field trips, introduce them to new hobbies and interests, and connect them with professionals in various fields. This exposure broadens students' horizons, sparks their curiosity, and encourages them to explore their passions.

By providing emotional support, developing coping mechanisms, and exposing students to new experiences, mentoring programs contribute significantly to their social and emotional development. Mentors serve as trusted guides who help students navigate the complexities of adolescence, build strong relationships, and make informed decisions. The positive impact of mentoring extends beyond the school years, as students carry the lessons they learn into adulthood, becoming well-rounded and contributing members of society.

Social-Emotional Learning (SEL) programs

SEL programs can take various forms and be implemented across different grade levels. They may incorporate classroom-based activities, small group discussions, and individual counseling sessions. Some common SEL strategies include:

- **Self-awareness**: Helping students identify and understand their emotions, strengths, and areas for growth.
- **Self-management**: Equipping students with strategies to manage their emotions, thoughts, and behaviors.
- **Social awareness**: Fostering empathy and understanding of others' perspectives and experiences.
- **Relationship skills**: Teaching students how to build and maintain positive relationships.
- **Responsible decision-making**: Providing frameworks for students to make thoughtful and ethical decisions.

Why now?

In the year 1995, I was a high school student, unaware of the significance of ACEs. During this era, there was a prevalent lack of understanding and recognition surrounding conditions such as Post-Traumatic Stress Disorder (PTSD), depression, and Attention Deficit Hyperactivity Disorder (ADHD) amongst others. Mental health discussions were often shrouded in stigma and misinformation, leaving many adolescents, including myself, unaware of the symptoms and effects of these conditions.

For many of us navigating the challenges of adolescence, mental health struggles were often dismissed or misunderstood. Symptoms of PTSD, stemming from traumatic experiences, were often attributed to mere mood swings or phases. Depression, characterized by overwhelming sadness and despair, was frequently brushed off as typical teenage angst. Similarly, the symptoms of ADHD, such as difficulty concentrating and impulsivity, were often overlooked or misinterpreted as behavioral issues rather than neurodevelopmental disorders. This lack of awareness had profound implications for individuals grappling with these conditions, myself included. Without the proper understanding and support systems in place, many of us struggled silently, feeling isolated and misunderstood. Seeking help for mental health concerns was often stigmatized, and resources for support were limited.

Thinking back on this time makes me realize how important it is to talk about mental health more openly and get rid of the stigma around it. It highlights the need for accessible resources and support systems within educational institutions and communities to address the mental health needs of adolescents effectively. By shedding light on conditions like PTSD, depression, and ADHD, we can create a more supportive and understanding environment for individuals facing these challenges, fostering empathy, resilience, and healing.

If only I had known about ACEs back then, it would have provided me with a much-needed framework to understand and navigate the challenges I faced. If only I had known about Adverse Childhood Experiences (ACEs) back then, it would have revolutionized my perspective and empowered me to navigate the challenges I faced. ACEs are a concept that elucidates the profound impact of childhood trauma on an individual's lifelong health and well-being.

Understanding ACEs would have provided me with a much-needed framework to comprehend the roots of my struggles. It would have been a revelation to recognize that my experiences were not isolated incidents but part of a larger pattern that affects countless individuals. Knowing that others have faced similar challenges would have instilled a sense of solidarity and diminished the feelings of isolation that I often grappled with.

Moreover, being aware of ACEs would have equipped me with valuable tools and strategies for coping with the consequences of childhood trauma. Instead of feeling lost and helpless, I could have sought out evidence-based interventions and therapies specifically designed to address the unique needs of individuals with ACEs. By developing a deeper understanding of the link between ACEs and their long-term effects, I could have proactively taken steps to mitigate their impact on my life.

Furthermore, having knowledge of ACEs would have empowered me to advocate for myself and others who have experienced childhood trauma. It would have given me the language and understanding to effectively communicate my needs and experiences to healthcare professionals, educators, and policymakers. By raising awareness of ACEs, I could have contributed to creating a more supportive and trauma-informed society that recognizes the importance of early intervention and prevention.

In retrospect, gaining knowledge of ACEs would have been a transformative experience that would have significantly altered the trajectory of my life. It would have provided me with hope, a sense of validation, and practical tools to heal and thrive despite the challenges I faced. While I may not have known about ACEs back then, it is never too late to learn and grow. Sharing my story and advocating for ACEs awareness is my way of ensuring that others do not have to navigate life's challenges alone.

The absence of awareness about ACEs left me navigating these challenges on my own, without the knowledge and support that could have made a significant difference. Reflecting on my own experiences, I can now recognize the role that ACEs played in shaping my mental health. It has given me a sense of validation and a deeper understanding of my struggles. While the past cannot be changed, armed with this knowledge, I am committed to fostering resilience and promoting healing within myself and others who have experienced childhood adversity.

The ACEs study has not only shed light on the impact of adverse childhood experiences but has also sparked a movement toward creating a more supportive and trauma-sensitive society. It serves as a reminder that we all have a role to play in ensuring that children grow up in safe and nurturing environments, free from the adversities that can have lasting consequences.

I wish I would have known about ACEs back in 1995! I wish I would have known that from my freshman year to my graduation day, ACEs had so much of an impact that led to depression and anxiety that I had to learn how to cope and manage on my own. School had its typical ups and downs, but I loved the opportunity to be a senior in high school. A glimmer of hope emerged when I received the news that I had qualified for graduation. This milestone held immense significance, as I was destined to become the first person in my family to graduate from high school.

The ACEs study has shed invaluable light on the profound impact of childhood experiences on our overall well-being. If only this knowledge had been available to me back in 1995, I might have had a better understanding of my own struggles and sought the appropriate support. Nevertheless, my journey as a mentor allowed me to make a positive difference in the lives of others, turning my childhood trauma into a catalyst for growth and resilience. Looking back, I realize that my passion for mentoring and supporting others stemmed from my own ACEs. Growing up in an environment marked by adversity taught me the importance of resilience and empathy. By becoming a mentor, I hoped to provide the guidance and support that I had craved during my own difficult times.

Mental health for students was not addressed in schools at that time. I never knew what depression really looked like. Prior to 1970, depression was viewed as a disorder for adults and was incorporated in the DSM-II in 19803 . My feelings were all over the place in high school, too. I honestly believe that my bond with some of my friends could have been because they had ACEs too! A few of my friends' parents lived in single-parent households or their parents separated and/or divorced so I understood the stories that they shared with me. Some students I grew up with committed crimes and were sent to juvenile detention; some students dropped out of school. I didn't realize until later that anxiety and depression was the reason why my oldest brother dropped out of high school.

In some school districts, positive interventions that support students with ACES are nonexistent because many teachers are not aware that ACES exists in their students' transition. Thus, this is one more reason why it is important for those students who can be identified with ACEs to get involved with EA. EA provides opportunities for cultivating interests and talents, introducing and developing interpersonal and life skills, gaining insight into competencies and passions, and broadening social capital and connections with peers and significant adults (Larson et al., 2004). Used as a tool, EA can promote relationships and environments that help children grow up to be healthy and productive citizens, thereby having the ability to build stronger and safer families and communities for their children.

When I decided to conduct my own research on ACEs, I did it based on my experiences growing up. My dissertation chair told me to choose a topic that I found of interest and that was when I started doing research.

---

3 - cdc.gov

At that time, I was the Director of Student Activities at my former school. I also became the mother of the building for some strange reason! Students started to come to me to talk about their life stories or share their stories about them growing up. I think that's the reason why a lot of students related to me because we shared the same experiences growing up. I realized that I could actually help them because I've already experienced some of the things that they had yet to experience, because I too have ACEs. The need to educate and address ACEs is at an all time high. I conducted research because I wanted to see if there was a relationship between ACES scores and participation in extracurricular activities (EA) in high school young adults. The research did show that those students that participated in extracurricular activities were better in school than those that didn't participate in EA.

As for my students, I noticed that they all stayed after school to participate in something because they never wanted to go home. Every year I came up with a different program or club that the students brought to me because they just wanted to be at school. They never wanted to go home. When they left their respective activities, they would go and participate in athletics. I noticed that there was more involvement with the juniors and seniors than the freshman. The students noticed it as well. In one of the clubs, they decided to create a "big brother, little brother" club where they incorporated the freshmen and made them feel welcome. I also noticed that other clubs started doing the same. From our marching band to the cheerleaders, it was an amazing sight to see!

Supporting an increase in student involvement in activities helped to create safe, supportive relationships amongst the students which lead to an increase in student achievement, improved student behaviors, and improved attendance. A lot of students did not even realize that I was a special education teacher because I interacted with so many students, ranging from the gifted and talented students to the severely profound, the commonality was student involvement.

Implications for Administrators

Principals should consider professional development for teachers to better understand ACEs. Once understanding ACEs becomes a part of professional development, teachers can be provided with the tools they need to implement ACEs initiatives in the classroom. A schoolwide social-emotional learning curriculum can help facilitate and support ACEs. The focus of most social-emotional learning programs is universal prevention and promotion—that is, preventing behavior problems by promoting social and emotional competence—rather than direct intervention. Social-emotional instruction can benefit every child, at every phase of development: those adapting well, those at risk, those beginning to participate in misbehaviors, and those already displaying significant problems. Another suggestion would be to visit schools and programs where ACES are being implemented to gather better understanding and help with implementation. Having classes during the school day as electives to support EA is another suggestion. Some schools offer classes such as choir, journalism, band, strength and conditioning, kinesiology, speech, which are just a few elective classes that are in schools that can gather student interest and teacher support found that electives allow students various opportunities to showcase their otherwise hidden strengths and talents to their teachers and their peers.

Principals need to consider professional development for teachers to encourage EA for their students. Some schools have EA before and after school. Many EA programs need to be reviewed and some EA programs need to be introduced and recommended by teachers who can support their students. If teachers support their students in their respective activities, it could change the culture and climate of the school, and it can bring a better level of understanding and respect for teachers and students. Promotion of EA can not only bring together environments through teachers who can foster student engagement inside and outside the classroom, but also can engage the community as witnesses to support the positive promotion that can benefit both the teachers and students.

Once principals complete the professional development of ACEs for teachers, implementation of ACEs and EA in the classroom can occur. Principals and teachers will never know how much of an impact the programs will be until they are tested. Testimonies of ACEs success stories will not only be a great benefit to all parties involved, they will allow everyone to listen first-hand to someone's experience. The more testimonies and exposure, the more that others will support. Other schools and districts will start gathering research for students in all grades and ages.

The overall goal is to support the primary prevention of ACES. School funding for EA is very important. More funding for EA can help the programs that are already in the school and possibly help teachers during school as well. The culture and climate is sure to change with more funding. Local officials and policy makers need to push the issue more because it would benefit more than the schools. More parents can be involved, and families can come and support. Providing support may be a great way to promote positive outcomes. EA is linked to several positive factors that can possibly develop into positive outcomes for our students.

Social- emotional learning and social-emotional support should take the lead in the education curriculum. For example, journal writing or art for students in the classroom are different ways for students to express themselves. Social promotion of EA as well as school funding for students K-12 and beyond should also be considered. Physical education is considered an EA. Having protective factors such as EA can be beneficial to the staff as well as all students who are faced with adversities. Used as a tool, EA can promote relationships and environments that help children grow up to be healthy and productive citizens.

Although no simple solution to ACEs exists, establishing a support system where collaboration takes place between family members and school staff is critical. This system should include children participating in EA and families supporting those events. The efforts could possibly impact those exposed to ACEs. EA can be used as one of many protective factors to support students struggling with ACEs . Having protective factors are important and creating protective factors that can be used in school can be beneficial to the staff as well as all students who are faced with adversities.

Whether it is abuse, neglect, or household challenges, ACEs have an influence on students. Recommendations for future research on ACEs suggest minimizing risks and assistance with preventing outcomes of adolescents with ACEs. Every school year, many students decide if they want to participate in EA. Research has shown that participation in EA can have a positive effect on students. Greater involvement in EA is associated with academic adjustment, psychological competencies, and positive peer context, a sense of identity, and student performance. ACEs research has shown that individuals who have been exposed to ACEs need positive interventions. The earlier that the interventions take place, the better chance that health related issues are minimal when they are adults. ACEs can have a lasting effect and a critical impact on the health of those students who are affected. Because of ACEs, many students are faced with health conditions such as stress and depression, two of the many reasons given when students are frequently absent or having discipline issues. The ACEs study has inspired other large-scale, risk-oriented CDC-sponsored health surveys such as The Family Health History, Health Appraisal Questionnaires and The BRFSS.

It's time to talk about ACES!

By creating victory among individuals through education and understanding ACEs is essential for several reasons:

1. **Breaking the Cycle of Generational Trauma:** Understanding ACEs allows individuals to recognize patterns of generational trauma and work towards breaking the cycle. By addressing and healing from ACEs, people can prevent the transmission of trauma to future generations, fostering a healthier family legacy.

2. **Promoting Empathy and Compassion:** Knowledge of ACEs fosters empathy and compassion among individuals. When people understand the impact of childhood trauma on others, they are more likely to approach relationships with understanding, patience, and empathy, contributing to a supportive and nurturing community.

3. **Enhancing Mental and Emotional Well-being:** Awareness of ACEs empowers individuals to prioritize mental and emotional well-being. By understanding the potential impact of childhood trauma on mental health, people can seek appropriate support, engage in self-care practices, and promote emotional resilience.

4. **Improving Parenting and Caregiving Practices:** Those who understand ACEs can apply this knowledge to enhance parenting and caregiving practices. Recognizing the effects of trauma helps individuals create a safe and nurturing environment for children, breaking the cycle of adverse experiences and promoting healthy development.

5. **Preventing Adverse Outcomes:** Knowledge of ACEs is instrumental in preventing adverse outcomes associated with childhood trauma. By addressing the root causes, individuals and communities

can implement preventive measures, reducing the likelihood of negative health, social, and behavioral outcomes.

6. **Creating a Supportive Environment:** Understanding ACEs contributes to the creation of a supportive environment. Communities that are aware of the prevalence of childhood trauma can develop resources, programs, and support networks to help individuals and families cope, heal, and thrive.

7. **Building Resilient Communities:** Addressing ACEs fosters resilience on an individual and community level. Through education, support, and intervention, individuals can develop the skills and coping mechanisms needed to overcome the effects of childhood trauma, contributing to the resilience of the entire community.

8. **Promoting Trauma-Informed Approaches:** Knowledge about ACEs encourages the adoption of trauma-informed approaches in various settings, such as schools, workplaces, and healthcare. This involves recognizing the prevalence of trauma, responding with sensitivity, and creating environments that support healing and growth.

9. **Reducing Stigma and Shame:** Open discussions about ACEs help reduce the stigma and shame associated with childhood trauma. When individuals understand that they are not alone in their experiences, it can lead to a more open and supportive dialogue, breaking down barriers to seeking help.

10. **Contributing to Collective Healing:** By creating victory through understanding ACEs, individuals contribute to a collective healing process. Shared knowledge, support, and empathy create a community that acknowledges the impact of childhood trauma and actively works towards healing and positive change.

So where should you begin? Take the ACEs Quiz!

Taking the ACEs quiz can be highly beneficial for several reasons:

Self-awareness: The ACEs quiz prompts individuals to reflect on their childhood experiences and assess the level of adversity they may have faced. This self-awareness can help individuals better understand the potential impact of their past experiences on their current health and well-being.

Identification of Trauma: Many people may not recognize certain experiences from their childhood as traumatic or adverse. Taking the ACEs quiz can help individuals identify and acknowledge past trauma, which is the first step towards healing and recovery.

Understanding Health Risks: Research has shown a strong correlation between ACEs and various physical and mental health outcomes later in life. By taking the ACEs quiz, individuals can gain insight into their risk factors for conditions such as heart disease, diabetes, depression, and substance abuse, among others.

Informing Treatment and Prevention: For individuals working in healthcare or social services, understanding a patient's ACEs score can inform treatment plans and interventions. It can also guide efforts in preventive healthcare by addressing underlying trauma and promoting resilience.

Empowerment: Knowing one's ACEs score can empower individuals to seek appropriate support and resources for healing. It can motivate them to engage in therapy, support groups, or other interventions aimed at addressing past trauma and building resilience.

Breaking the Stigma: Taking the ACEs quiz helps normalize conversations around childhood trauma and adversity. It breaks down the stigma associated with discussing sensitive topics and encourages open dialogue about the impact of early experiences on health and well-being.

Advocacy and Policy Change: Understanding the prevalence and impact of ACEs in society can inspire advocacy efforts and policy change aimed at preventing childhood trauma and supporting individuals affected by it. By raising awareness and sharing their ACEs scores, individuals can contribute to broader initiatives for social change and trauma-informed care.

In summary, taking the ACEs quiz is a valuable tool for self-awareness, identifying trauma, understanding health risks, informing treatment and prevention, empowering individuals, breaking stigma, and advocating for policy change. It promotes a greater understanding of the impact of childhood experiences on lifelong health and well-being, ultimately contributing to individual and collective healing. Creating victory among individuals through understanding ACEs is a transformative journey that not only promotes personal healing but also contributes to the well-being of communities. It is a step towards breaking the cycle of generational trauma, fostering empathy, preventing adverse outcomes, and building resilient, supportive ents for individuals to thrive.

It is time to talk about ACES!!!

It is time that we all raise awareness about ACEs and their profound impact on individuals' lives. As part of my commitment to promoting understanding and support for those affected by ACEs, I will continue to:

- **Increase Awareness:** I will share information and resources to educate our community about the prevalence and consequences of ACEs.
- **Foster Compassion:** By sharing stories and testimonials from individuals who have experienced ACEs, in the hope to foster empathy and understanding among our community members.
- **Provide Support:** I will highlight resources, support services, and organizations that offer assistance to individuals and families affected by ACEs.
- **Advocate for Change:** I will advocate for policies and initiatives aimed at preventing ACEs, supporting survivors, and promoting resilience and healing.

How can you help:

You can help by sharing our resources with your networks, and engaging in conversations about ACEs and trauma-informed care. Together, we can create a more supportive and compassionate community for all. Thank you in advance for your support and commitment to raising awareness about ACEs and supporting those affected by trauma.

Be Victorieus!

--Dr. Torie

Take the ACEs quiz to get started on your ACEs Educational journey:

https://forms.gle/MNhfV8JBzVGGpDoG8

Be Victorieus Podcast has been going strong for 2 whole years! It's streaming on all podcast platforms. Check us out on YouTube as well:

https://youtu.be/emOUr4hyF1o

Join me and share your ACES story with me!

https://calendly.com/bevictorieuspodcast/
be-victorieus-virtual-podcast-interview

APPENDIX A: REFERENCE

Williams, E. P. (2019). *Examining the relationship between the findings from Adverse Childhood Experiences Questionnaire and participation in extracurricular activities in young adults.* Chicago State University

APPENDIX B: LIST OF SERVICES

The Center for Disease Control and Prevention (CDC) has provided a list of resources available should you need services.

CDC's Division of Adolescent and School Health (DASH)

DASH strives to prevent serious health risk behaviors among children, adolescents, and young adults. The division also offers many resources on preventing violence in schools.

Measuring Violence-Related Attitudes, Behaviors, and Influences Among Youths: A Compendium of Assessment Tools [PDF 6.01MB]

This compendium provides researchers and prevention specialists with a set of tools to assess violence-related beliefs, behaviors, and influences, as well as to evaluate programs to prevent youth violence.

A Comprehensive Technical Package for the Prevention of Youth Violence and Associated Risk Behaviors [PDF 4.09MB]

This technical package is a compilation of a core set of strategies to achieve and sustain substantial reductions in youth violence. Technical packages help communities and states prioritize prevention activities based on the best available evidence. This package is intended as a resource to guide and inform prevention decision-making in communities and states.

National Centers of Excellence in Youth Violence Prevention

CDC's Division of Violence Prevention funds five National Centers of Excellence in Youth Violence Prevention (formerly, Academic Centers of Excellence). The purpose of the Centers is to reduce youth violence in defined high-risk communities by implementing and evaluating a comprehensive strategy to prevent youth violence. Centers work with researchers, local organizations, and a high-risk community to reduce youth interpersonal violence. Centers monitor youth violence, support the development and application of effective youth violence prevention programs, and mobilize and empower communities to address youth violence. Centers serve as local, regional, and national resources for developing and applying effective evidence-based prevention strategies in communities.

STRYVE

STRYVE is a national initiative led by the Centers for Disease Control and Prevention (CDC) to prevent youth violence. To realize its vision—safe and healthy youth who can achieve their full potential as connected and contributing members of thriving, violence-free families, schools, and communities—STRYVE is working to increase awareness that youth violence can and should be prevented, promote the use of youth violence prevention approaches that are based on the best available evidence, and provide guidance to communities on how to prevent youth violence. STRYVE helps communities take a public health approach to preventing youth violence—stopping it before it even starts.

Youth Violence Training and Technical Assistance Center

CDC has established a new Youth Violence Training and Technical Assistance Center (YVTTA) via a cooperative agreement with the American Institute of Research. The YVTTA will develop tools and resources to assist 12 local public health departments and their community partners coordinate and implement youth violence prevention approaches that are part of their comprehensive plan.

Federal Resources

CrimeSolutions.gov

The Office of Justice Programs' CrimeSolutions.gov is a U.S. Government website that categorizes the research on what works in criminal justice, juvenile justice, and crime victim services.

Youth.gov

Youth.gov is the U.S. government website that helps users create, maintain, and strengthen effective youth programs. Included are youth facts, funding information, and tools to help users assess community assets, generate maps of local and federal resources, search for evidence-based youth programs, and keep up-to-date on the latest, youth-related news.

National Criminal Justice Reference Service

This service offers an extensive source of information on criminal and juvenile justice, providing a collection of clearinghouses supporting all bureaus of the U.S. Department of Justice, the Office of National Drug Control Policy, and the Office for Victims of Crime Resource Center.

National Gang Center

The National Gang Center is a collaborative effort between the Office of Justice Programs' Bureau of Justice Assistance and the Office of Juvenile Justice and Delinquency Prevention. This web site features the latest information about anti-gang programs and links to a wide range of resources.

Office of Juvenile Justice and Delinquency Prevention—Model Programs Guide

The Office of Juvenile Justice and Delinquency Prevention's Model Programs Guide (MPG) is designed to assist practitioners and communities in implementing evidence-based prevention and intervention programs that can make a difference in the lives of children and communities. The MPG database of evidence-based programs covers the entire continuum of youth services from prevention through sanctions to reentry. The MPG can be used to assist juvenile justice practitioners, administrators, and researchers to enhance accountability, ensure public safety, and reduce recidivism. The MPG is an easy-to-use tool that offers a database of scientifically-proven programs that address a range of issues, including substance abuse, mental health, and education programs.

Office of Juvenile Justice and Delinquency Prevention—Strategic Planning Tool

The Strategic Planning Tool is a resource that encompasses four interrelated components to assist in addressing a community's gang problem. Those components link descriptive information about risk factors, best practices, strategies, and research-based programs. Communities can catalogue existing local resources by creating a Web-based Community Resource Inventory account accessed on this tool.

The Office of Juvenile Justice and Delinquency Prevention

The Office of Juvenile Justice and Delinquency Prevention (OJJDP) provides national leadership, coordination, and resources to prevent and respond to juvenile delinquency and victimization. OJJDP supports state and community efforts to develop and implement effective and coordinated prevention and intervention programs. OJJDP also seeks to improve the juvenile justice system so that it protects public safety, holds offenders accountable, and provides treatment and rehabilitative services tailored to the needs of juveniles and their families.

Safe Schools/Healthy Students Initiative

The Safe Schools/HS Initiative is a unique Federal grant-making program designed to prevent violence and substance abuse among our Nation's youth, schools, and communities. This comprehensive approach to Youth Violence Prevention is administered through the Substance Abuse Mental Health Service Administration, part of the U.S. Department of Health and Human Services.

Stopbullying.gov

Stopbullying.gov lists information and federal resources on how to identify and prevent bullying.

United States Secret Service — National Threat Assessment Center, Safe School Initiative [PDF 1.6MB]

In 2004, the Secret Service completed the Safe School Initiative (SSI), a study of school shootings and other school-based attacks. Conducted in collaboration with the U.S. Department of Education, the study examined school shootings in the United States as far back as 1974, through the end of the 2000 school year, analyzing a total of 37 incidents involving 41 student attackers. The study involved extensive review of police records, school records, court documents and other source materials, and included interviews with 10 school shooters. The focus of the study was on developing information about the school shooters' pre-attack behaviors and communications. The goal was to identify information about school shootings that may be identifiable or noticeable before such shootings occur, to help inform efforts to prevent school-based attacks.

Additional Online Resources

American Psychological Association

The American Psychological Association and MTV (Music Television) are encouraging young people to become proactive in identifying the warning signs of violent behavior in themselves and their peers.

Center for the Study and Prevention of Violence / University of Colorado at Boulder

The Center for the Study and Prevention of Violence works from a multidisciplinary platform on violence to bridge gaps between the research community, practitioners and policy makers. An Information House collects research literature on the causes and prevention of violence and provides direct information. In 1996, the Center initiated a project to identify violence prevention programs that met high scientific standards of program effectiveness and could provide the foundation for developing a national violence prevention initiative. The results, Blueprints, describe 11 practical and effective violence prevention programs that have effectively reduced adolescent violent crime, aggression, delinquency, and substance abuse. Another 18 programs have been identified as promising programs.

Children's Defense Fund / Education and Youth Development Division

The goal of Children's Defense Fund's Education and Youth Development Division is to give every child a safe start in life. The Division does so by identifying and promoting programs and policies that keep children out of trouble, protect them from violence, and provide them with a safe and productive learning environment.

Children's Safety Network / National Injury and Violence Prevention Resource Center

The Children's Safety Network provides resources and technical assistance to maternal and child health agencies and organizations seeking to reduce unintentional injuries and violence toward children and adolescents. This is one of four Children's Safety Network Resource Centers funded by the Maternal and Child Health Bureau of the U.S. Department of Health and Human Services.

National Archive of Criminal Justice Data

The National Archive of Criminal Justice Data facilitates and encourages research in criminal justice. It does so by preserving and sharing data resources and providing specialized training in quantitative analysis of crime and justice data.

The National Gang Crime Research Center

The National Gang Crime Research Center exists as a non-profit independent agency with the mission statement to: (1) Promote research on gangs, gang members, and gang problems in cooperation with federal, state, and local government agencies; (2) To disseminate up-to-date valid and reliable information about gangs and gang problems through the official publication of the NGCRC, the Journal of Gang Research, and, (3) To provide training and consulting services about gangs to federal, state and local government agencies.

National Mental Health and Education Center

This public service program of the National Association of School Psychologists provides resources for safe-school programs and crisis response and offers information on current issues and programs.

National School Safety Center

The Center provides training materials on school crime prevention and safe-school planning to educators, law enforcers, and other professionals who work with youth. Educational information is also provided for parents.

The Prevention Institute Urban Networks to Increase Thriving Youth through Violence Prevention

Urban Networks to Increase Thriving Youth through Violence Prevention (UNITY) is a national initiative designed to strengthen and support cities in preventing violence before it occurs and to help sustain these efforts.

DR. TORIE'S INSPIRING JOURNEY

From Adversity to Achievement

In the heart of Kansas City, a tale unfolded, woven with threads of resilience and determination. Dr. Torie, a woman marked by the shadows of Adverse Childhood Experiences (ACEs), faced the formidable challenge of severe depression and anxiety throughout her formative years. School and everyday challenges seemed insurmountable, yet a flicker of strength burned within her.

As Dr. Torie navigated the tumultuous waters of adolescence, she recognized the transformative power of education. By her senior year, a realization dawned upon her – she was destined to become the first in her family to graduate from high school. This revelation sparked a deep-seated commitment to ensuring others could follow in her footsteps. At the tender age of seventeen, Dr. Torie began mentoring freshmen in Kansas City, guiding them through the maze of academic and personal challenges. Little did she know that this act of mentorship would become the cornerstone of her life's work.

Her educational journey led her to the University of Central Missouri in Warrensburg, where she graduated with a Psychology degree despite a challenging GPA. Driven by an unyielding dream to become the first doctor in her family, she knew she had to return to school. After a short term residency in Indianapolis, the bustling city of Chicago became her new home. In Chicago, she embarked on a multifaceted journey. Dr. Torie started as a substitute teacher, balancing the demands of academia, family, and personal aspirations. Her resilience shone brightly as she earned a Master of

Business Administration, celebrated the arrival of her first baby girl in 2006 and successfully graduated with a Master of Arts in Teaching In 2008. Dr, Torie's family expanded, as did her determination to complete her goals.

Four years later, with another baby girl in her arms, Dr. Torie continued her ascent. She took over the role of Director of Student Activities, proving that dedication could indeed shape a remarkable career. However, she harbored an unfulfilled dream – a dream that lay in the halls of academia. The opportunity arose when Dr. Torie gained acceptance into the doctoral program at Chicago State University. It was here that she chose to delve into the intricate relationship between Adverse Childhood Experiences and participation in extracurricular activities in young adults.

As the Director of Student Activities and a mother of three, Dr. Torie undertook the daunting task of pursuing her doctorate degree. In a culmination of dedication, hard work, and a passion for understanding, she examined the nuances of ACEs and extracurricular engagement. The fruits of her labor manifested as she earned her doctorate, becoming the first person on both sides of her family to receive her doctorate degree!

Dr. Torie's journey is a testament to the transformative power of education, mentorship, and unwavering determination. Her story echoes through the halls of inspiration, inviting others to defy the odds and reach for their dreams, no matter the challenges they face.